Ha!

Other Peter Kreeft books from St. Augustine's Press

Ecumenical Jihad: Ecumenism and the Culture War

Ethics for Beginners: Big Ideas from 32 Great Minds

I Surf, Therefore I Am: A Philosophy of Surfing

If Einstein Had Been a Surfer: A Surfer, a Scientist, and a Philosopher Discuss a "Universal Wave Theory" or "Theory of Everything"

Jesus-Shock

Ocean Full of Angels: The Autobiography of 'Isa Ben Adam

Philosophy 101 by Socrates: An Introduction to Philosophy via Plato's Apology

The Philosophy of Jesus

The Platonic Tradition

Sea Within: Waves and the Meaning of All Things

Socrates Meets Descartes: The Father of Philosophy Analyzes the Father of Modern Philosophy's Discourse on Method

Socrates Meets Freud: The Father of Philosophy Meets the Father of Psychology

Socrates Meets Hume: The Father of Philosophy Meets the Father of Modern Skepticism

Socrates Meets Kant: The Father of Philosophy Meets His Most Influential Modern Child

Socrates Meets Kierkegaard: The Father of Philosophy Meets the Father of Christian Existentialism

Socrates Meets Marx: The Father of Philosophy Cross-examines the Founder of Communism

Socratic Introduction to Plato's Republic

Socratic Logic 3.1e

Summa Philosophica

Ha!
A Christian Philosophy of Humor

Peter Kreeft

St. Augustine's Press

South Bend, Indiana

Manufactured in the United States of America.

1 2 3 4 5 6   27 26 25 24 23 22

Library of Congress Control Number: 2022940027

Paperback ISBN: 978-1-58731-318-9
Ebook ISBN: 978-1-58731-319-6

∞ The paper used in this publication meets the minimum requirements of the American National Standard for Information Sciences – Permanence of Paper for Printed Materials, ANSI Z39.48-1984.

St. Augustine's Press
www.staugustine.net

Contents

Introduction

I have been teaching philosophy full time for 62 years. I have taught over 500 classes and given over 500 public lectures. I never give the same class or lecture twice because I have ADD and get bored very easily, especially with myself. Out of all of these talks, the one that got the best, most enthusiastic response by far was the one I gave recently, for the first time, on the philosophy of humor, at the University of Dallas. I told the audience it was a test run for a possible book, and their appreciation may have been colored by that and by their politeness, but I don't think people can tailor the depth and loudness of their laughter by politeness.

According to God's book, there is "a time to weep and a time to laugh" (Ecclesiastes 3:4). The surest sign that our culture is in deep doo-doo is that we are increasingly sure that this is a time to weep and increasingly doubtful that it is a time to laugh. Another sign is that our Presidents no longer dare to use phrases like "deep doo-doo." An even worse sign is that we are not *allowed* to laugh if we are in danger of being politically incorrect or unwoke or of "offending" anyone who has a paper-thin skin and a leather-thick heart.

This book almost didn't exist. I was about to write a serious, heavy book entitled *How To Save Western Civilization*, as a sequel to my book *How To Destroy Western Civilization and Other Ideas from the Cultural Abyss*. But writing it was not making me happy, and reading it was not going to make anybody else happy either. And then I stopped just long enough for my guardian angel to squeeze through that tiny window of opportunity that I had opened up by my silence and to whisper this commonsense question into my subconscious: "Why not make them happy instead?" (Angels specialize in common sense.)

I started thinking: Western civilization is neither healthy, happy, nor holy. Humor is all three.

Humor is not only holy, it's Heavenly. And if you are surprised to be told that humor is Heavenly, you need to read this book because you reveal your misunderstanding of both humor and Heaven. If you ask, "Is there laughter in Heaven?" my answer is: "You can't be serious!"

C.S. Lewis wrote that "joy is the serious business of Heaven." We sink into quicksand when we don't take ourselves lightly.

Many of us are obsessed with culture and civilization and politics. We have no king but culture. We'd like to convert the culture even though we can't even convert ourselves.

If you are obsessed with politics, please remember that the meaning of "politics" has two parts. The first part is from the Greek word "poly," meaning "many," and the second part is ticks, which are annoying little bloodsucking bugs. There will be no politicians in Heaven, but there will be humor. No one will worship either the donkey or the elephant, they will worship a Lamb instead. (That is one of Heaven's many jokes.) And the Lamb refused to run for office when he came here. Instead of running for it, he ran *from* it, from those who wanted to make him king (Jn 6:15).

Harry Truman once said: "In this great land of ours, every baby that's born an American citizen can grow up to be President some day. That's just the chance the poor little bastard has to take."

Of course we need to address our decadent and dying culture's crisis. And because the crisis is at root spiritual, not economic or racial or political or environmental, because the battlefield is the human spirit, therefore this is a spiritual warfare, and fighting on the side of the angels here is honorable and necessary. "Culture warriors" are *warriors* (unless the Supreme Court has reversed the law of non-contradiction). But warriors don't need to be hard and heavy like battleships and tanks and cannons. They can also be light. A butterfly in the eyes of a tank commander can determine the outcome of a battle. Remember the angels, God's air force. Chesterton says "angels fly because they take themselves lightly." Perhaps some of the bombs of God's air force are jokes.

So perhaps a book like this could be more help in winning the culture wars than books about the culture wars. Hundreds of other people are philosophizing about how to save Western civilization, but who is philosophizing about humor? And of those few, how many write books you can laugh at? Most philosophies of humor are deadly serious—which is a great joke in itself.

I am a philosopher, but this is not a typical philosophical book, that is, a humorless, scholarly, serious book. The book itself is only a little more than an excuse to make you laugh by sharing my favorite jokes with you, in the Appendix. And even in the "serious" part of the book, it's not scholarly. I deliberately avoided doing research in books or libraries or the Internet about theories of humor. I have no theory of humor to top or replace those of other thinkers. This book is neither a better philosophy of humor to replace and transcend all existing ones, nor is it a synthesis of existing ones, a "survey." It's not factual or historical. In fact its main purpose is not even theoretical but practical: it is to make you laugh, and thus to make you happy.

Many philosophers distinguish between two different points of view, or two different kinds of knowing, or two different purposes in thinking. The following dualisms or distinctions or polarities are all similar though not quite identical.

The distinction exists in many languages: "kennen" vs. "wissen" in German, and "connaitre" vs. "savoir" in French.

Bertrand Russell distinguishes between "knowledge by acquaintance" and "knowledge by description."

Gabriel Marcel distinguishes between "mysteries," in which we are personally involved, and "problems," in which we are not.

Michael Polyani distinguishes between "personal knowledge" and impersonal or scientific knowledge.

C.S. Lewis distinguishes between "looking-along" and "looking-at."

Aristotle distinguishes between "practical" and "theoretical" knowledge.

We also distinguish between the arts and the sciences. We don't expect artists to be scientific and we don't expect scientists to be artistic.

The medievals distinguished between "active" and "contemplative" knowing as well as between the active life and the contemplative life.

Pascal distinguished between "the intuitive mind" and "the geometrical mind," and between the "heart" and the "head." The "heart" was not just feeling but a form of reason, for "the heart has its *reasons* that the reason does not know."

The reason is abstract, the heart, or intuitive mind, is concrete.

Let's call these two the Peter-mind and the Paul-mind. Both saints exemplified both, but Peter was more concrete and practical than Paul, and Paul was more abstract and theological than Peter. Popes have to lead and rule, which is practical; that's why not many popes were philosophers or theologians.

Most philosophies of humor rob Peter to pay Paul. I refuse to do that, because I AM Peter. Literally, I mean. In terms of my job, I am Paul: I teach philosophy.

But not here. My title is not simply "A Philosophy of Humor." There are many philosophers of humor, and many philosophies of humor. And every one of them is wrong somehow.

They are not wrong to do it, to try it, but they are wrong to expect it can be done, to claim success. Why? Because humor cannot be reduced to any other terms, or explained in any other categories, or reduced to any other concept, or analyzed into any number of parts.

For some, its essence is irony (Kierkegaard). For some, it's class envy and resentment (many Marxists). For some, it's tension-relief (Freudians and many materialists). For some, it's the deflation of the ego (Chesterton). For some it's the refutation of static stubbornness (Bergson).

Each of these factors is present in humor, so it's not wrong to say "Humor is x, or y, or z." But it's wrong to say that x or y or z is humor, or the essence of humor. All humor is x and y and z but not all x or y or z is humorous. Work that out for yourself with every x or y or z you can find.

The point is that humor is sui generis. It is not reducible to its parts or to an essence or to one of many examples of a genus or class concept. Nor is it analyzable into its parts. It cannot be assembled out of its parts, like a machine. It is more like an organism, which is more than the sum of its parts. More like a person, like you.

If you've come this far with me, come one more step. We have seen that the question most philosophers ask about humor—define it, tell me its essence—is unanswerable. Not because it is unreal or subjective or totally relative or undetectable, but because it is like music, or language, or religion: a fundamental dimension, a fundamental category. Now the next question, the real question, is: Why do we try? Why do we want to do this? Why pin the butterfly to the page? Why "murder to dissect"? What motivates this Ockhamist reductionism of the marvelous to the pedestrian, the complex to the simple, the mystery to the problem, the whole to its parts ? Why are we in love with this "will to power" over everything, even our concept of laughter, which we enjoy for its power *over us*?

I do not answer that question for you. Look in the inner mirror and answer it for yourself.

The purpose of this book is to not to make you an "expert" on humor but a humorist to make you like Chesterton's angels, which fly because they take themselves lightly. Wouldn't you rather fly than understand the technology of flight?

Popes (Peters) are often funnier than theologians (Pauls). Pope John XXIII had a sharp sense of humor. Two stories exemplify that. One, well known, is his answer to the question he got from many tourists, "How many people work at the Vatican?" His answer was "About half."

The other was the story about the workers who were sandblasting the papal apartments, not knowing the Pope was inside. One smashed his sander against his hand and drew blood. He swore, in Italian, "Mother of God!" The Pope heard it and stuck his head out the window. The sandblaster apologized, "Oh. Sorry, Holy Father. I didn't know you were there." The Pope asked, "Are you a Catholic, my son?" "Yes, Holy Father." "Is your mother still alive?" "Yes, Holy Father." "So you know you have a mother on earth. What is her name?" "Lucia, Holy Father." "Do you use her name as a swear word? Do you say 'Lucia!' when you are angry because something bad happens to you?" "Oh, no, Holy Father." "Then why do you use the name of your Mother in Heaven as a swear word?" "Well, Holy Father, when you have pain like this, you can't just say 'Ouch!' You have to say something stronger." "Yes, that is very true. I understand. But you should not use something good and beautiful as a swear word, but something bad and ugly. I will teach you how to swear. I know nine languages. I will teach you how to say 'shit' in nine languages." And he did.

Even the first half of this book, the philosophical and theological half, tries to be Petrine as well as Pauline. Even though it talks about humor as an abstract object, a universal, an essence, rather than just presenting concrete particular existing examples of it (jokes), its aim is not to solve the riddle about what humor is and why it makes us laugh, but just to explore it—like the Japanese mountain climbers who beat the Americans to the peak of K2, the world's second highest mountain, but came back down having stopped fifty feet from the summit even though the weather was perfect. When the Americans asked them why they did that, they replied, "You climbed K2 to conquer the mountain; we climbed to befriend it." Humor is a large mountain; let's befriend it instead of conquering it.

A few of the jokes in this book I invented myself, a few more I found in print (jokes are not copyrighted), and most of them I just heard from the grapevine, and the grapes tasted good.

That's a good image because listening to jokes is like wine tasting. When someone shares a really good one with you, you have to pass it on. Jokes, like biological life itself, are meant to be passed on. Like the institution of the family, jokes are part of the "pay it forward system." It's God who invented both families and jokes, of course, and that's His very essence: self-giving. And that's why that's the meaning of life for us who are created in His image: sharing, loving, turning every getting into a giving, passing it on. We can't unscrew our hearts but we can un-Scrooge them.

Jokes are not the only form of humor, of course, but they are to humor what parables are to moral wisdom: they are very short *stories*. Stories are the oldest and most universal of all human arts. No human culture, however primitive, has ever existed that did not tell stories. And no animal species tells stories. We tell stories because our lives themselves are stories. Story telling as well as philosophy is a "know thyself." We tell stories because we *are* stories. The Bible is a story before it is theology, morality, liturgy, prophecy, etc., all of which are commentaries on the story.

What kind of story is life? That's a great way of asking the philosophical question "What is the meaning of life?" It was Sam's way of asking the greatest of questions, in *The Lord of the Rings*, when, on the way to the Crack of Doom, he mused to Frodo, "I wonder what kind of story we're in?"

There are three good answers to that question: Life is love, life is war, and life is a great joke, and invitation to laugh.

I've read a lot of books about humor, and in every one of them I looked first for the jokes, i.e., for the things that would actually make me laugh rather than the philosophical passages that would make me understand laughter.

You will probably like the Appendix better than the book, even if you like the book and even if you don't like all the jokes in the Appendix, because jokes are more fun than philosophizing about jokes. If you had to choose between them, which of the following would you choose? Would you rather I told you a joke and make you actually laugh, or told you my philosophy of why you laugh? Would you rather go to Heaven or go to a great lecture on Heaven? Would you rather fall in love or read a book about falling in love?

Understanding is tremendously important, but so is happiness. Both are non-negotiable goods. But which would you choose, if you had to choose: to experience happiness or to understand it?

It's true that understanding is one of the things that can make us happy, and it's also true that true happiness can help us to understand. Both are means to each other, and both are also ends and not just means. We want to understand just because we want to understand, and we want to be happy just because we want to be happy.

So I'm writing this book first of all to make you a little happier, and also, I think, secondarily, a little wiser and more understanding. The book is like a thread on which I string some pearls. The pearls are the jokes and the thread is the philosophy. Most books on humor seem to love the threads more than the pearls, if we judge by how much space they allot to each.

Philosophy and jokes should not be alien to each other, for the point of philosophy ("the love of wisdom") is wisdom, and the point of jokes is laughter, and both wisdom and laughter serve the same end, namely human happiness. And I mean by "happiness" not the shallow, modern meaning of mere subjective satisfaction but in the deep, classical sense of "eudaimonia": objectively true completion, fullness of being, flourishing. We are not complete, not completely real, if we lose our sense of humor.

Here are seven of the greatest and most mysterious things in life. They are also seven of the things that make us the happiest:

1. beauty
2. mystical experience
3. romantic love
4. music
5. humor
6. sanctity, i.e. genuinely self-forgetful altruistic love
7. wonder and worship in adoration of God

These are seven essential and not accidental properties of human beings that distinguish us from all the other animals. As Chesterton said, "alone among the animals, man is shaken with the beautiful madness called laughter." Many philosophers and scientists have written about all five of these properties, but no philosopher has ever given an adequate explanation of any one of them. They are all mysterious, and express themselves para-doxically, by tears that weep and laugh at the same time, like Sam Gamgee's foretaste of Heaven at the end of *The Lord of the Rings:*

"And…to Sam's final and complete satisfaction and pure joy, a minstrel of Gondor stood forth, and knelt, and begged leave to sing. And behold! He said: '…I will sing to you of Frodo of the Nine Fingers and the Ring of Doom.' And when Sam heard that he laughed aloud for sheer delight, and he stood up and cried, 'O great glory and splendor!'…And then he wept. And all the host laughed and wept, and in the middle of their merriment and tears the clear voice of the minstrel rose like silver and gold, and all men were hushed. And he sang to them, now in the elven-tongue, now in the speech of the West, until their hearts, wounded with sweet words, overflowed, and their joy was like swords, and they passed in thought out to regions where pain and delight flow together and tears are the very wine of blessedness."

We are that host who laugh and weep together. We weep because Tolkien's art has done its highest and holiest task: it has broken our hearts. C.S. Lewis wrote: "Have you not seen/ In all our days/ Of any human work or art,/ Our truest and sincerest praise/ Means, when all's said, 'You break my heart'?"

When the heart breaks, blood and water flow out. (Cf Jn 19:34.) When we laugh, we become fluid. And we overflow our container. The container is the self. The self, paradoxically, cannot contain itself. It has overcome the most serious law of all, the logical law of identity, that a thing is itself, that X is X, and not non-X. But sometimes X *is* non-X, and that's hilarious! Of course I don't understand it. That would spoil it.

Michael O'Brien writes about a scene in his life that is emotionally very similar to the scene from the end of *The Lord of the Rings* quoted above. He was there at the birth of each of his children, and "As each child was born, I surprised myself [surprise is an essential ingredient in humor] and my wife too—we both spontaneously burst into tears and laughter simultaneously [now that's really a spiritual "simultaneous orgasm!"]—tears and laughter and shouts of joy, even though there had been so much pain. It was not articulated, there were no words for it. It was an eruption [like a volcano, or like an orgasm] from the heart and soul, a condition of awe before this phenomenal mystery which had come into our hands, this little person who had come from our love."

There had been pain. The comedienne Carol Burnett says, "If a man wants to understand what giving birth feels like, he should take his lower lip and stretch it over his head." But childbirth *disproves* Vin Scully's cynical comment about sports: "Losing feels worse than winning feels good." Maybe that's true in sports, but the opposite is true in life.

The Greek word "hilarion" means "joy," but also humor, the hilarity of laughter. It happens only at rare and precious moments in this world. I am pretty certain that it happens much more in the next.

Babies are closer to that other world than we are because they laugh at everything. They laugh at every *thing* because they laugh at *Everything*. They are good philosophers, because philosophy at its rarest and highest is about that "Everything." When we see babies laughing at Everything, we laugh too if we are wise and humble enough to let ourselves be instructed by their divinely inspired wisdom.

*

This book is probably not one of the best books in the world on the subject, but its subject is one of the best things in the world. That's why it's worth reading. Aristotle, the philosopher of common sense, noted that even a little knowledge of the greatest things makes us happier than a lot of knowledge of lesser things. To "know thyself" is one of those greatest things, and humor can often give us crucial aspects of self-knowledge that nothing else can.

That's a heavy thought, but in this light book I won't drop that heavy thought on you because——Oops, I can't finish that sentence because I just *did* drop that heavy thought on you, and all I can do about it now is to ask your forgiveness and hope we can laugh together at my self-contradictory stupidity. "The jury will please disregard that remark of the last witness," but of course it can't, because in order to disregard anything we have to know what thing to disregard, and that means to regard it.

My straight and serious point is that this book is not at all straight and serious. Perhaps it's not a very good book at all, but only a good joke on itself; but, then, a good joke often makes you happier than a good book, at least for a few precious seconds.

A good joke turns us into Shakers. It makes us *shake* with laughter. It's like a mental orgasm. It *is* a mental orgasm. We are out of control, we are in the playing hands of Higher Forces, like a kitten in the hands of a juggler. In the words of the old romantic Hollywood cliché, "it's bigger than both of us."

Sexual orgasm is joy in the body. Mystical experiences, out-of-the-body and out-of-the-ordinary-mind experiences, are joy in the spirit. Good jokes are joy in the mind. Like those other two experiences, they are *ecstatic* in the literal sense: "ek-stasis" means "standing outside yourself." Good jokes help us to stand outside ourselves and transcend ourselves, for they make us laugh *at* ourselves, as if we are someone else. That is paradoxical. The self or "I" is the subject, not the object; and when our object is the self, we stand outside ourselves. When we laugh at ourselves, the laugher and the laughed-at become one. We overcome the dualism of ordinary subject-object consciousness. It is like a mystical experience.

Psychologically, we are doing three things. We are transcending our categories and concepts and mental expectations our mind; we are transcending our choosing and controlling desires in our will; and we are transcending our everydayness and ordinariness and boredom in our emotions. And that is a kind of magic that very few other things can do. I know of only the seven I listed above. Humor is in great company!

*

The most brilliantly intelligent and profound religious philosopher of all time, who was also a canonized saint, did not finish his masterpiece, the *Summa Theologiae*, the greatest book of theology ever written, because, he said, in light of the mystical experience he had, that everything he had ever written looked to him like "straw." The joke is that straw was used in his culture to cover animal dung, in-cluding the anal product of horned bovines. That's my candidate for the best philosophical joke in history.

But, Professor, are you really seriously saying that about your philosophy too, about your own chosen profession and vocation and high calling? Is most of philosophy a cover for a pile of skubala? (It's the Greek S-word, and it's in the Bible, so there! Look it up: Philippians 3:8.)

My answer: Are you really serious in asking that question?

But…but…but God is serious, and therefore so is theology, and therefore so is philosophy.

Indeed they are. And so are we, since God created us in His own image. Which means that our sense of humor, as well as our seriousness, is an image or pale copy of His. After all, He designed the ostrich, the otter, and the octopus. Have you ever watched them carefully? The art reveals the Artist!

But somehow that seems a little sacrilegious.

No. What verges on sacrilege is to deny God's sense of humor, not to affirm it.

But….

You have too many buts.

*

Our Christian faith is totally centered on Christ, on what Chester-ton called "that single paradox, that the hands that had made the sun and stars were too small to reach the huge heads of the cattle (in Bethlehem's manger). Upon this paradox, we might almost say upon this jest, all the literature of our faith is founded. It is at least like a jest in this, that it is something which the scientific critic cannot see. He laboriously explains the difficulty which we have always defiantly and almost derisively exaggerated, and mildly con-demns as improbable something that we have almost madly exulted in as incredible, as something that would be much too good to be true, except that it is true. When that contrast between the cosmic creation and the little local infancy has been repeated, reiterated, underlined, emphasized, exulted in, sung, shouted, roared, not to say howled, in a hundred thousand hymns, carols, rhymes, pictures, poems, and popular sermons, it may be suggested that we hardly need a higher critic to draw our attention to something a little odd about it; especially one of the sort (of critics) that seems to take a long time to see a joke." (*The Everlasting Man*)

Telling a good joke makes someone laugh, and making someone laugh is an act of charity. Therefore being a good comedian is a high and holy calling.

We can even perform this act of charity toward God. How can you make God laugh? Just tell Him your plans.

Being a Christian allows you to laugh at *everything* for two opposite reasons. The first is because everything, even evil, is working together for good to all who love God the omnipotent, omniscient, and omnibenevolent One who works out all things for our good (Rom 8:28). That is the positive laughter, the laughing *with* all things. The second is the negative laughter, the laughing *at* all things, all things that we used to take seriously as our false gods, our false absolutes: life, death, pleasure, pain, health, disease, honor, dishonor, satisfaction, dissatisfaction, poverty, wealth, donkeys, elephants, and even most kinds of love, all the world's pitiful moralistic or legalistic or emotionalistic or ideologistic substitutes for *agape*, the self-forgetful, self-giving love that goes all the way up into ultimate reality as the very essence of God.

The first laughter, the positive laughter, is the laughter of Susan and Lucy Pevensie as they ride Aslan the resurrected but definitely *not* tame lion, who, they now know, is indeed the Lord of the whole world. The second laughter, the negative laughter, is the laughter of the freed, free-flying fly, at the spider whose web is now empty. "He that sitteth in the heavens shall laugh." In fact laughter puts you in the heavens with Him, as do those other six things.

The first, philosophical, half of this book is simply a few small contributions to a philosophy of humor. It is also a theology, and a distinctively Christian one, because its author cannot tell lies and pretend to be neutral toward the Great Paradoxical Joke that is the meaning of all things. That paradox is not something he looks *at* but something he looks *with,* or looks *along.* More accurately it is not some*thing* but some*one,* who is among many other things the Greatest Comedian Who Ever Lived.

In the first half of this book we will look at the relation between humor and thirteen of the most important things in human life: health, happiness, holiness, goodness, truth, beauty, suffering, time, morality, philosophy, theology, mysticism, and Jesus. It will make you laugh less than the second half will, because philosophizing about humor is less humorous than humor itself, just as cook books don't taste as good as food. So there is no good reason why you should not read the second part first. But the first part, the philosophical part, should contribute to your happiness too because good philosophy is almost as important as good jokes.

1. Humor and Health

What good is humor? It's healthy, happy, and holy. Those are the three levels of life, and humor helps them all. Humor is also hearty, high, humble, homely, human, helpful, hopeful, heavenly, heart-warming, heartbreaking, hedonistic, haphazard, and hilarious.

Why do so many of its attributes begin with the letter H? I don't know; I didn't design either the world or the alphabet.

Health is the good of the body, happiness is the good of the soul, and holiness is the good of the spirit. Health is our right relationship to the material world, happiness is our right relationship to our own and others' selves, and holiness is our right relationship to God.

Humor is healthy in four ways.

First, it is a cause of physical health. It sends good chemicals into the brain. It makes you happy, and that makes you healthy. (Soul moves body as well as vice versa.) All other things being equal, the longer you laugh, the longer you live. If we never stopped laughing, we'd never die. OK, that's not quite true, but at least we'd die laughing.

Second, it is not only a *cause* of physical health but also an *effect*, and thus a *sign*, of physical health. Sick people laugh less than healthy people.

Third, it is also a cause of *mental* and moral and spiritual health. This is because it makes you happy, and when you are happy you are not usually doing destructive and evil things, but good things. If you doubt that, ask any sane psychologist. (Yes, some psychologists are quite sane. Even some philosophers are.)

16

Fourth, it is also an *effect* of mental and moral and spiritual health. People lacking in mental and moral and spiritual health don't laugh much; and when they do, it resembles that of hyenas.

There are even some very materialistic philosophers who claim that there is no difference in kind between hyena laughter and human laughter. This fact leads me to the uncomfortable but inevitable conclusion that some philosophers who live outside mental institutions are more seriously disturbed mentally, morally, and spiritually than the patients who live inside them.

That's all I have to say on the subject, and therefore I will do what writers almost never do: I will shut up about it. Wittgenstein wrote a whole terribly logical book (the *Tractatus Logico-Philosophicus*) just for the sake of the last sentence: "Whereof one cannot speak, thereof must one be silent." ("Wovon man nicht reden kann, davon muss man schweigen.") That whole book was taken so seriously that Cambridge University gave him a professorship on its basis alone, without any other scholarship or writings, and the University did not realize that it was one very large joke, perhaps the longest one in the history of philosophy, a spectacularly successful "shaggy dog story."

So I will learn Wittgenstein's lesson and be silent, remembering that God often answers our wordy questions with a "Shut up and dance with Me," which is essentially what He said to Job. But I will not just shut up, I will also make a big, splashy, wordy point about shutting up. I will not shut up about shutting up. I will be like Hamlet, who said, "I am dead, Horatio!"—which is also a great joke, because dead men do not speak. Hamlet is the joke on Descartes: the living self-contradiction of an existing individual claiming he does not exist. It can be done! Hamlet did it.

The next time I confront something I want to avoid, I think I shall simply forget to exist. I am an absent-minded professor: that should be easy for me.

Another joke on poor Descartes is the proof that, although he was a genius, Descartes should not be ranked as greater than a horse, because as everyone admits, you shouldn't put Descartes before the horse.

See? Even stupid jokes can make us a little happy for a little while. And that is my next point.

2. Humor and Happiness

"Comedian" is a high and holy calling because comedians make people happy. Good comedians love three things: laughter and happiness and people. Bad comedians love money or fame or misery or anger.

I am a philosopher and a college professor. "Philosophy" means "the love of wisdom." The French word for "lover" is "amateur." The opposite of "amateur" is "professional." College professors like myself are professionals. We sell our work. We philosophers get paid for philosophizing, that is, for being lovers of wisdom. So we are professional lovers. We all know the word for "professional lover." It begins with the letter p. I am an intellectual prostitute. No one would be foolish enough to buy my body, but some are foolish enough to buy my mind. Boston College is my pimp.

Most of us have mixed motives in almost everything we do. No one knows how many professional comedians love money more than laughter, or happiness, or people, just as no one knows how many professional philosophers love money more than wisdom. But amateur comedians, as distinct from professional comedians, make no money from their comedy, so they have to love laughter for its own sake, simply because it makes people happy.

What is a laugh? A laugh is simply a big smile. A smile is simply a little laugh. A smile is to a laugh what a baby is to an adult. A teenager is halfway there. A single-syllable half-laugh like "heh" is like a teenager, confused by being caught halfway between childhood and adulthood. More than a smile, less than a laugh.

Smiles are the most obvious sign of happiness, even to a new-born baby who can't understand a single word. When you smile at him, he smiles back at you; when you frown at him, he frowns back or cries. Everyone understands that smiles are the most natural and instinctive and ineradicable sign of happiness. Except the "experts" at the Global Happiness Project, who every year rate the five Scandinavian countries as the happiest in the world and the countries in sub-Saharan Africa as the least happy in the world, even though Africans smile the most and Scandinavians smile the least. (How often do you hear "those smiling Scandinavians" or "those sour, dour Africans"?) Only an "expert" on happiness could possibly forget what even a newborn baby knows: that smiles are the surest signs of happiness. There are some ideas that are so absurd that you have to have a PhD to believe them.

Commonsense logic would teach us that if smiles are the signs of happiness and if Africans smile more than Scandinavians, Africans are happier. But experts don't measure the size of smiles but of bank accounts. Sub-Saharan Africa is the poorest subcontinent in the world, and Scandinavia is the richest. So we have two empirical facts, which cannot be denied: that Africans smile the most and that Africans are the poorest. The conclusion that logically follows from these two premises is something like the wisdom taught by Jesus, Buddha, Socrates, and all the saints and sages, namely that poverty is a blessing, or at least an opportunity for happiness, and, correlatively, that wealth is a curse, or at least a great danger to happiness. That's almost a "Duh!" You have to be very clever to cover that up.

Here is another empirical fact: Scandinavia has one of the highest suicide rates of any subcontinent, and sub-Saharan Africa has one of the lowest. Similarly, the suicide rate for individuals is usually much higher among the rich than among the poor. So naturally the Global Happiness Project picks the Scandinavian countries as the happiest and the countries in sub-Saharan Africa as the unhappiest. Just as smiles are the most obvious indication of happiness—to everyone but an "expert"—so suicide is the most obvious indication of unhappiness—to everyone but an "expert." In their very failure to reveal others, the "experts" reveal themselves. Note that, and thank them.

Isn't it ironic how "experts" with no sense of humor can stimulate ours? How people who don't laugh are laughable? How those who don't *tell* jokes *are* jokes?

3. Humor and Holiness

Humor not only helps make us healthy and happy, but it even helps make us holy. And besides those three things, what else is there?

To see the connection between humor and holiness, remember that we can look at humankind only from three points of view: (1) the human, (2) the sub-human, and (3) the super-human.

(1) If we look at humans from the human point of view, two things will probably happen. The first is that we will be confused because we will get in our own way. Whenever we claim to have succeeded in the Socratic project of "know thyself"—whenever we say to ourselves, "There I am"—we will be mistaking the object for the subject, mistaking "There I am" for "Here I am," mistaking the image that the mind projects onto its inner movie screen for the projecting mind itself. The one thing it's impossible to be non-subjective about is subjectivity. Knowledge is like light. Light itself cannot be a lit object. We can know rocks because we transcend rocks, we escape being rocks, we are not rocks; but we cannot know ourselves because we do not transcend ourselves, we cannot escape ourselves, we cannot not be ourselves. "Know thyself" is a Zen koan puzzle, a Catch-22. Only God can know us. We are Hamlet; that is why we do not know ourselves. Only Shakespeare knows Hamlet. The secret of our identity is not within us or below us but above us.

The second thing that will happen if we look at ourselves from our own point of view is that we will probably take ourselves much too seriously, because the ego is a pufferfish.

This gives me the opportunity to tell a joke about that ego. It's only a second-rate joke (which is pretty good in a world of third- and fourth-rate jokes) but it's psychologically and theologically significant.

Let me tell you the real story of Adam and Eve. God created Eve first, and she was lonely, and God said to her, "I've got a great surprise for you. It's a man." "What's a man?" asked Eve. "Oh, you'll love him, and he'll fall madly in love with you, and you'll make lots of little people in the most delightful way, and he'll do all sorts of things for you like opening stuck jar lids." "Sounds too good to be true," Eve replied, "so what's the catch?" God answered, "Well, he's going to have a big ego. So I'm going to have to tell him a little lie: that I created him first. And you're going to have to play along with it. Do you promise?" "I promise," said Eve, and smiled that Mona Lisa smile that she's been smiling ever since.

Adam's version of that joke is that God created him first, and he was lonely, so God said, "I've got a great surprise for you. It's a woman." "What's a woman?" asked Adam. "Oh, you'll fall madly in love with her. She's my masterpiece, the most beautiful thing in the universe. And you'll make lots of little people with her in the most delightful way, and she'll love you back, and adore you, and obey you, and follow you, and believe everything you tell her, and never even bitch at you." "Wow," said Adam. "That sounds too good to be true. What's the catch?" "And God answered, "Well, there's a price tag. It'll cost you an arm and a leg." And Adam said, "What can I get for a rib?"

No apologies to those who don't get the joke because they're Biblically illiterate. They're like the people who don't get the joke about Judas Iscariot being the first Catholic bishop to accept a government grant. Or the one about the Bible being all about baseball, starting with the big inning. Or—I think I'll stop here.

(2) Since looking at ourselves from our own point of view is so problematic, let's try the second possibility: let's look at ourselves

from the sub-human point of view, e.g., the point of view of a cat or a dog or a mosquito. A cat thinks of us as its slightly retarded pet, a dog thinks of us as its mysterious and wonderful god, and a mosquito thinks of us as her meal. (Only female mosquitos bite.)

Eve has been trying on those three animal costumes in her relationship with Adam throughout human history, and this has contributed to the confusion. Especially since Adam loves to wear the costumes of wolves, vampires, or gorillas.

It should be obvious that more can't be understood or explained by less, only vice versa. Animals don't understand us as well as we understand them. Apes don't write psychology books.

(3) So the only possibility left is the superhuman point of view. Since we do not know the minds of angels or the existence of extraterrestrials, the only hope is a God's-eye point of view.

Which we don't have. (Stop the presses! Call out the reporters!)

But Jews, Christians, and Muslims believe that God has revealed to us a tiny part of His infinite mind; and one tiny part of that tiny part is His sense of humor. Psalm 2:4 says, "He that sitteth in the heavens shall laugh." At us His toddlers flopping around like drunken penguins trying to walk on ice.

So the first answer to "know thyself" is that we are God's jokes.

Just as we make art because we are art, and just as we make children because we are children, so we make jokes because we are jokes.

To laugh at ourselves is a delightful and easy aid to holiness. In fact, though it is far from sufficient, it is necessary. That ego has to be deflated, like tires on sand dunes. Holiness, or sanctity, requires virtues; and the very first and most necessary virtue of all is humility, which is the alternative to the worst sin of all, the sin of Satan, namely pride, arrogance, playing God. St. Augustine, asked to name the four cardinal virtues, replied: "Humility, humility, humility, and humility."

But humility is usually misunderstood. It's not a low opinion of yourself; it's *no* opinion of yourself. It's self-forgetfulness, to the point of being able to laugh at yourself as a joke. Proud people always think and talk about themselves. Humble people don't want to talk about themselves, and that's also why they're happy. Sometimes proud people talk about how bad they are, and that's a form of pride too, a dangerous one because it's camouflaged.

Humility is the pin that deflates the balloon of egotism. Jokes are both causes and effects of humility. They both foster and express humility.

How? By their *surprise*. The secret of most jokes is the timing, the sudden "aha!" moment. If you see that coming, the joke doesn't work, it isn't funny. A joke is funny only if and when you are turned upside down and realize that you had been standing on your head—which is the funniest posture of all, and one it's impossible not to laugh at.

You were standing on your head because you were making the wrong assumption from the one in the world of the joke. You laugh at yourself as Senator Ed Muskie laughed at himself during his Democratic campaign for President when he was about to speak to a field of Republican farmers in Iowa and discovered that they had forgotten to build him a platform to stand on. So to make himself visible to thousands of farmers in a totally flat landscape, he hopped on the tallest thing he could find, a piece of farm equipment. He asked what it was, and they told him it was a manure spreader. So he began his speech by saying, "For the first time in my life, I find myself giving a Democratic speech from a Republican platform."

The worst thing Job ever says is, "I stand on my integrity." (Job 27;5, 31:6) That's standing on a manure spreader.

Rodney Dangerfield says, "When you're looking out for Number One, you're going to step on lots of Number Two." And that's what "he that sitteth in the heavens will laugh" at.

"Humble" is etymologically related to "humus," or earth. Humility brings us down to our common earth and off our high horse. So does humor. What humility is to all the other virtues, humor is to humility: first among servants.

Jesus, Socrates, Confucius, and Lao Tzu all had a great sense of ironic and humble humor. Alexander the Great, Genghis Khan, Ivan the Terrible, Napoleon, Hitler, Stalin, Pol Pot, and Mao Zedong did not.

Humility is the deflator of pride, the greatest sin. All sins involve some pride, some inflating of ourselves into gods and some deflating of God into ourselves.

The two most essential truths we need to know are the two things God said to St. Catherine in a mystical vision, the two things that summarize all of divine revelation: "I'm God, you're not." My favorite sermon, the shortest and the funniest. The joke's on us.

What's so incredibly funny (and also incredibly tragic) about that short sermon is that we keep forgetting that second point.

The way humor makes us humble is that when we laugh, we lose *control.* We lose control not only over our mind and our expectations but also over our own body. A laugh is like a fit, a fart, a burp, a hiccup, or a sneeze, none of which we want to do when we are giving our acceptance speech for being elected to high office. Humor unravels and removes our mask, our persona, which means literally that artifice through ("per") which we sound ("sona") our lines in our play-acting.

Look at the simplest and crudest form of humor: a man who takes himself very, very seriously slipping on a banana peel. Notice that even though we are laughing *at* him rather than *with* him, our laughter necessarily partakes of the same temporary loss of control in our own body as the thing we laugh at, namely his loss of control in *his* body. We shake at his shaking, and in so doing we are willy nilly laughing *with* him, not just *at* him.

This undermining of our control is a form of irony. Irony is the contrast between reality and appearance, or between reality and our expectations. Expectations are our attempts at controlling reality, especially future reality, by our thoughts, or at least controlling the gap between reality and our thoughts.

That was probably the most un-funny, abstract, and philosophical paragraph in the whole book so far. But don't give up on it yet.

In the example of the egotist and the banana peel, there is a double irony. The first is the contrast between the egotist's "upright" position in his own mind and his "down and dirty" prone position in reality. The second is the contrast between our attempt to laugh *at* him for losing body control and the loss of *our own* body control in the act of laughing.

Humor pricks pride's balloon, rains on pride's parade. As Chesterton says, "pride is the gorgon." Pride is the fault we find the most obvious and the least tolerable in others. It is also the fault we find the least obvious and the most tolerable in ourselves. (And isn't *that* ironic?) Proud people usually think of themselves as humble and humble people think of themselves as proud. Sinners think they are saints and saints think they are sinners, just as fools think they are wise and the wise think they are fools. Which one do you think is more likely to be right?

Humor is holy because it is Godlike, for God has the best sense of humor of all. He turns us all upside down. "He has put down the mighty from their thrones and exalted those of low degree; he has filled the hungry with good things and the rich he has sent away empty." (Lk 1:51-53) This from the one who knew him best.

And when God gave us his most perfect and complete self-revelation, and became one of us, it was not as a wizard or a warrior or a king or an elf but something like a hobbit. Or perhaps "the killer rabbit" in "Monty Python and the Holy Grail." He is also Mary's little lamb. What a disguise!

To see the holiness of humor we should look at it from God's holy point of view. God certainly has a sense of humor. Does God also have a philosophy of humor?

There are many different philosophies of humor, but the commonest one and probably the best one centers on irony, paradox, surprise, and role reversal. And this seems typical of God. For instance, for his "triumphal entry" into Jerusalem on Palm Sunday, Jesus chose to use not a stallion, as all great conquerors did, but a jackass. And he has been choosing members of the same species to do his work ever since.

It takes a certain kind of mind to understand irony, or at least why irony is funny. Perhaps the central joke in the Bible comes at the end, in the highly symbolic book of Revelation, where the Last Battle is between two symbolic animals. Jesus is pictured as a Lamb ("arnion"—the word means not just "lamb" but "wee little lambkin"), and he is warring against the Dragon ("therion"—the most terrible of monsters—the Devil, of course). The battle is for the heavyweight championship of the universe and the salvation of the human race. When we look at the two contestants we think this is a fixed fight, and we're right; but we're also wrong, because it's the Lamb who wins. In fact he most definitively *whups* the Dragon. How? Because he has a secret weapon that the Devil can neither understand nor withstand: his own blood.

One of the lines of the "Anima Christi" prayer is: "In thy wounds hide me." The Devil can enter and pervert Christ's powers in the world, but he can neither enter nor pervert Christ's wounds, his sufferings, either in Christ himself or in us, Christ's body. When we experience the sufferings God allows the Devil to put into our lives and accept them in faith and trust and offer them to Christ for his work of salvation, the Devil withdraws, because he sees that the very thing he invented to harm us and weaken us and destroy us is strengthening us. That becomes true of all sufferings, especially the last and most total one, death.

From the human point of view, what happened to Christ on

the Cross was the most terrible defeat and the most terrible suffering and the most terrible evil that ever existed; but from the divine point of view it was so good a trick of spiritual judo, using the enemy's own strength against him, that Christians celebrate it on a holiday they dare to call "*Good* Friday." God turned the greatest evil into the greatest good. The most terribly serious thing that ever happened is also God's supreme joke on the Devil.

Mel Gibson got the joke. In his movie "The Passion of the Christ," we hear a terrible groan of pain come up from the ground at the moment Jesus dies on the Cross. That was the Devil being tricked by the divine judo. Judo uses the enemy's own force against him, arranges for him to defeat himself; and "the bigger they are, the harder they fall." God turned His enemy and His enemy's instruments (Judas, Pilate, Herod, Caiaphas, the Romans) into His own instruments. God used the Devil and the Devil's instruments to save the world from the Devil.

That's a great joke from God's point of view, and "he that sitteth in the heavens shall laugh." But we do not sit in the heavens, so we do not laugh, because from our human point of view what happened on Calvary was the most terrible and serious thing that ever happened.

But we can also look at it, and all sufferings, from God's point of view, because He has shared that point of view with us, by divine revelation. And that's why we can even joke about it, as the martyrs often do as they die (St. Thomas More said: "Axeman, I prithee spare my beard; it has not committed treason against King Henry"; and St. Lawrence, roasted on a barbecue, said, "Please turn me over, I'm not done on the other side yet.") And we can believe, even if we do not feel, that Saint Theresa was right when she said that the most painful life on earth, looked back on from the heavenly point of view, will appear as no more than one night in an inconvenient hotel. God's joy and glory and triumph swallows up the worst the Devil could do as the sea swallows up a grain of sand.

To use still another image for the irony in the Christian Gospel, the very dam of death that seemed to stop the river of life, on the Cross, was so conquered and swept away by the current that it became part of that river.

It's the same story Tolkien told in *The Lord of the Rings*. That book is not an *allegory* of the Gospel, but it has *the same plot* because Sauron was tricked by the same joke, the same secret weapon of self-sacrificing love, as Satan was. Remember the joy Sam and Frodo had when they completed their task of destroying the Ring of Power. (Actually, it was Gollum who destroyed it: an irony within the irony!) Their joy and satisfaction even *before* they were rescued in the end was the same that Job got even *before* God gave him all his "stuff" back again. Jesus, Job, and Frodo were in the same story. The score of all three games was God 1, Satan 0.

Of course that triumphant joke does not mitigate the horror of the Crucifixion, the supreme evil in history, the torture and murder of the God of love; it *presupposes* it. The Resurrection presupposes the death; the deliverance from evil presupposes the evil; the joy presupposes the sorrow. As the joke presupposes the seriousness from which the joke delivers us.

And what happened to Jesus is not an exception, but the rule. Because Jesus is not the exception but the rule: he reveals not only who God is but also who we are and what our lives are. And he makes all our evil, all our suffering, and all our passion part of the same story as his, the same irony, the same joke. He makes "*all* things work together for good for those that love God" (Romans 8:28), because all the things in our lives are in that story. Our history is his story. The meaning of history is missing from all the secular history books. And that's also supremely funny, supremely ironic.

Humor is not only holy but also Heavenly, a foretaste of Heaven. When we are suddenly relieved of some terrible burden, we laugh with relief. Part of the meaning of that laugh is that we laugh at the heavy seriousness with which we took that burden that is now lighter than air. That's an anticipation of Heaven's peace, which makes us laugh at our silly little wars with God, and at ourselves for not fully realizing the simple truth that "in his will is our peace" (the line from Dante that T.S. Eliot called the greatest line in literature). We laugh with God even at our sins, once they are gone. They are like hemorrhoids.

*

We've looked at humor's healthiness, happiness, and holiness. That covers everything because we have only three dimensions: body, soul, and spirit; the physical, the psychological, and the religious; the world outside us, the world within us, and the world above us.

Some forms of Hinduism and Buddhism deny the first of those three worlds, the world below us, and say that that material world is nothing but a projection of the mind, either ours or God's. That philosophy is the subject of a fairly famous joke:

A guru had a reputation for great wisdom. One day his students saw him in a very unedifying and compromising position: he was running as fast as he could down the street being chased by a herd of thundering wild bull elephants. One of his students cried out to him, "Master! Remember what you have taught us! Those elephants are not real! Stop running." The guru, without missing a step, called back, "Who's running?"

Atheism, of course, denies the third world, the super-human world, and says that we created God in our own image rather than vice versa. That's like saying that Hamlet invented Shakespeare. So why didn't Hamlet invent a Shakespeare who wrote only comedies, not tragedies like the one poor Hamlet was in?

I know of no one who denies the middle world, the world of thinking; because thinking that one does not exist can be done only by thinking. Horses and carts may be only dreams, but dreams require dreamers. That's why we must put Descartes before the horse.

Buddha came close to denying the middle world by denying the substantiality of both the individual ego ("jiva") and the collective ego ("atman"), but he could not deny the thinking process itself. He could deny only a thinker behind the thinking. But that seems as hard to believe as denying the existence of a killer behind a killing—which is why you don't find many successful Buddhist defense attorneys. It's like denying a taxer behind your taxing, i.e., denying the existence of the IRS. That may be an attractive philosophy on April fifteenth, but it is refuted (and also, incidentally, proves the existence of a refuter) not by the laws of logic but by the laws that will put you in prison for tax evasion.

Most of us believe in the existence of, and seek the goods of, all three worlds: health, happiness, and holiness. One of the things that gives us a sudden injection of all three H's is humor. So you have three reasons to keep reading this book.

4. Humor and Truth

Truth, goodness, and beauty are the three things (1) that we all want, (2) that we all want the most, (3) that we all want without limit, (4) that never bore us, and (5) that satisfy our three soul-powers or spiritual powers of mind, will, and heart that distinguish us from all other animals. The thinking mind is satisfied by truth (there are many kinds of truth); the choosing will is satisfied by goodness (there are many kinds of goodness); and the desiring heart is satisfied by beauty (there are many kinds of beauty).

Humor operates most clearly in the realm of the mind and truth.

The truth we all need and want the most is more than just *facts*; it's *understanding*, especially understanding about ourselves and our lives. And as Socrates understood better than anyone else in his world, Lesson One among these truths that we need to understand is the understanding that we lack understanding; the wisdom to know that we are unwise. (That in itself is very funny, although we are usually too serious and egotistic to laugh at it. And that gives us an even sillier second thing to laugh at!)

Socrates also believed that we innately but unconsciously do know these most important truths, but that we have forgotten them, and he tried to unearth these unconsciously known universal truths by his famous Socratic method of systematic logical questioning. Humor does the same thing as the Socratic method: it reminds us both of how stupid we are (because we don't know we're stupid) and also how wise we are (because deep down we do know these things, we've just forgotten them). That is how humor works.

The "punch line" does the same two things to us, like the answer to a riddle.

We need to look more specifically at just how humor can teach us important truths about ourselves and our lives more effectively than all the sciences, including philosophy.

Remember what we said above about the essence of most humor being irony, which is the contrast between objective reality and what we subjectively know or expect to know with our minds or see with our eyes. Humor shocks us out of our ignorance. Advice, preaching, moralizing, and research try to do that too, but they can't do it nearly so quickly, or shockingly, or delightfully, as humor can. We don't usually laugh with delight at a good sermon, but we can't help laughing at a good joke. We also remember the joke better than the sermon, because it gives us an "aha!" experience of truth. It is like the surprise of a sudden jab of a sharp pin rather than a long, vague, inner ache.

Here's a humble example:

An old curmudgeon orders soup in a restaurant, does not eat it, and calls the waiter over.

"Is anything wrong, sir?"

"Yes, there is. I want you should taste this soup."

"If you don't like it, I'd be happy to bring you another kind of soup."

"I don't want another kind of soup."

"Well, what do you want?"

"I want you should taste my soup."

"I can't do that, sir, but I can happily bring you something else, whatever you like."

"No, I want you should taste my soup."

"Sir, you are a very persistent customer. Please tell me what is wrong with your soup. This restaurant is committed to satisfying all of its customers."

"You can satisfy me only if you taste my soup."
"Oh, all right, if you insist. Let me see…where is the spoon?"
"Aha!"

What happens here, both in the mind of the waiter and in the mind of the person who hears the joke, is what psychologists call "the 'Aha!' experience" or "the 'Eureka!' experience." It is the moment of revelation, the surprise, the unexpected. We laugh because we are "tickled." A tickle is a gentle shock. Here it is given the mind instead of the body. A less gentle shock would be a pain, but a slight shock is a joy.

So humor does what love does: it transform pains into joys. Imagine you are a knight. Fighting dragons out of fear of their fire is not a joy for you, but a necessity or a duty. But fighting dragons out of love for your lady fair is a joy. Doing a difficult task for a tyrannical boss is a pain, but doing it for your lover is a joy.

One more such sudden surprise:

A tourist whose watch had stopped working was walking through the Jewish section of Warsaw looking for a watch repair shop. Finding a little storefront with no sign but with a big watch in the window, he rang the bell. An old Jewish man came down and asked, "What do you want?" "I want to get my watch fixed. You fix watches, don't you?" "No. I do circumcisions. I am a mohel." "Oh. Sorry. Why do you have that big watch in your window then?" "So what do you think I should put in my window, eh?"

The key to most jokes is the timing, the surprise, the unexpected answer. And the "eh" at the end. It often consists in role reversal. The classic example of this role reversal is the classic Jewish joke:

"Why does a rabbi always answer a question with another question?" And the answer is: "So tell me, why *shouldn't* a rabbi answer a question with another question, eh?"

Actually, this joke reveals something quite profound about Jesus, who was, of course, a rabbi. Jesus almost never answered a question with the expected answer, but instead by that same role reversal. The reason he did that was not just a psychological trick; it was an ontological inevitability, since God incarnate is God, and God is the "I AM" and we are His "thou" rather than vice versa. We habitually think we are the "I" and God is our "thou." In other words we habitually think inside out and upside down. We use the divine name "I" for ourselves and we call God the "other," the object. But when we meet the real God, the questioner (ourselves) becomes the questioned one, and the questioned one (God) becomes the questioner; and when this happens, we get a glimpse of the real relationship between ourselves and God, which will become inescapable at the Last Judgment. The role reversal of humor enables us to escape this escapism for a second.

For we are all like Job: we want to put God in the dock and ourselves on the judge's bench. And when God answered Job, it was with the question: "Where were you when I designed you and your life? I didn't notice you there with the angels giving Me advice about how to design your life." It was a far better answer than the most complete theodicy could ever have been. It is also very funny to see Hamlet giving Shakespeare advice about creative writing.

Humor, like religion, changes our perspective. It lets us look at ourselves, our smallness, and our foolishness, from God's perspective. And that is shattering. For God is infinite—literally and actually infinite, not just potentially infinite, or unlimited, like the series of positive numbers or like the space of an ever-expanding universe, but actually infinite in all perfections. Thus from God's point of view this whole unimaginably immense universe is less than a grain of sand. Lady Julian of Norwich saw it as a tiny hazel nut in God's hand. For infinity dwarfs *any* finite quantity infinitely more than any finite quantity, however great (like the number of subatomic particles in the universe), dwarfs any finite quantity, however small (like the size of the smallest particle).

And *that*, and nothing less, is the God who became a zygote, and a baby, and a corpse, and what looks like a piece of bread— out of love for us, for you. If this God is for us, who can be against us? Poor Satan and his minions. A mere lamb defeats him, child of a human woman, who herself drives him to terror more than trillions of angels do.

Isn't that an incredible joke?

Of course jokes in themselves cannot hold or teach that tremendous truth, that enormous enlightenment. But they teach its corollary: the smallness of our darkness. In the punch line of a good joke, one of the things that surprises us and delights us, despite ourselves, is the discovery of our own smallness, silliness, or stupidity. And that delights us as well as shaming us. For there are *two* deep desires in our mind: to know and not to know this small- ness; to run into that light and to run away from it. And a good joke always invites us to rejoice in that light that shows us up, to laugh at ourselves. In that way a good joke is an anticipation of the joy of Heaven. By showing us our smallness it shows reality's largeness. It is the contrast between those two things that is ironic and funny. Neither the light of truth in itself nor the darkness and ignorance in itself is either ironic or funny; but the juxtaposition of the two is.

Here is another example of a similarly delightful downer or put-down:

A priest, a minister and a rabbi were friends. They all had in common a love of animals and an admiration for Saint Francis of Assisi, who not only preached to the birds but also tamed a wild wolf. Each one thought he was the one who had the most of Saint Francis's spirit. One day they decided to resolve that dispute by a contest. They want camping in the woods, and each was to find a bear, tame him, convert him, and bring him back to their camp. The minister came back first with a bear that he had taught to pray the "sinner's prayer" on his knees. The priest came back next with a bear that he had baptized. The rabbi came back last, but without a bear and with his clothes ripped and his skin bleeding. "What happened to you?" they asked. The rabbi said, "It's not fair! You Protestants have to start with the sinner's prayer, and you Catholics have to start with baptism, but we Jews have to start with circumcision."

A Catholic version of the bear joke has the same kind of punch line, the real world breaking in on our expectations:

A pious Catholic thought he had the spirit of Saint Francis of Assisi, so he want out to convert a bear. It didn't work because the bear he picked was angry and hungry, and it attacked him. He started running away, but the bear ran after him. He soon saw that he couldn't outrun the bear, so he thought that at this point his only hope was a miracle. So he stopped running, knelt, and prayed, "God, I can't do this but you can. Please convert this bear and make him a good Catholic." He turned around and saw that his prayer was being answered, since the bear had also stopped running and was kneeling and praying. "Thank you, Lord!" the man said. And then he heard what the bear was praying: "Bless us, O Lord, and these Thy gifts, which we are about to receive through Thy bounty."

This bear joke is really a man joke. It exposes ourselves and our follies. Folly is funny. Humor is a way to "know thyself." We tell jokes because we *are* jokes.

In Lewis's Narnia creation story in *The Magician's Nephew*, he shows us the genesis of humor when Aslan explains to the Jackdaw who has unwittingly made the first joke, "You have not *made* the first joke; you have only *been* the first joke." And all the animals laughed at the Jackdaw (who is us), as the bear laughed at the

Catholic in the joke, and as God laughed at Baalam with a horsy hee-haw. (Cf. Num 22: 21-35)

We find animals funny (especially on "America's Funniest Videos"), but they would have more reason to find us funny, if they only had a sense of humor. At least they manifest God's incredible sense of humor: did you ever see a gooney bird landing?

The following animal joke was so famous that its punch line was deliberately and cleverly slipped into many of the episodes of "Doc Martin," a beloved and successful British comedy series about a curmudgeonly doctor who incidentally hated dogs. (That was a joke within a joke because Martin Clunes, who played Doc Martin, was famous for his love of dogs.)

Ethan and Evan were two curmudgeons who lived next to each other in the Maine woods. They never visited each other or even talked to each other. One day Ethan learned that Evan was dying, so he thought he ought to break their silence and visit him before it was too late. The problem was that Evan always had an enormous black dog chained to his front porch who growled threateningly at anyone who passed. So Ethan walked over to Evan's house and shouted, from a safe distance, "Evan, it's Ethan! Can I come in?" "Ethan? Why the hell do you want to come in?" "Because I heard you're dying, and I wanted to say good-bye." "Oh. Well, O.K. Come in." "But won't your dog bite me?" "No, he won't." "You sure?" "Yep." "Promise?" "Promise." So Ethan walked up to the porch and the dog attacked him viciously. Now he's all torn and bleeding, and when Evan opened the door, Ethan complained to him, "You promised your dog wouldn't bite me. Look what he did!" Evan looked at the dog and answered: "That ain't my dog."

All these jokes are about truth. And the truth common to all of them is that truth is not what we expect. Jokes suddenly tear through the little frames of our pictures, the pictures we make in our minds about what things are and what will happen next. And this is both disconcerting and delightful, as I noted above (p. 26).

As Michael O'Brien says, "humor is the delight of suddenly expanded perspective. Humor is the transformation of linear vision into the multidimensional. Humor is not logical, Nor is it antilogical. It is meta-logical."

Or one might say that humor is logical and shows us that we are not. But it is best to say that humor is neither logical nor illogical (i.e., *less* than logical) but trans-logical (*more* than logical). It is like love that way, and beauty, and music, and mysticism.

"Philosophy" means literally "the love of wisdom." Wisdom is a form of truth, the highest kind of truth, not truth about trivia but truth about ourselves and about the most important things in life. And that is also a definition of good humor.

5. Humor and Goodness

And since that expanded perspective gives us both wisdom and humility, and since wisdom and humility are essential parts of human goodness, humor gives us not only truth but also goodness.

Humor prods us to virtue by exposing the stupidity of vices. When we laugh at our stupid sins, we side with God rather than the Devil. The Devil hates the sound of that laughter.

There are plenty of examples of good jokes that fight against spiritual or moral evil by doing to our pride (the master vice, the most dangerous sin) what a pin does to a balloon. One of them is the joke that was voted "the best joke of the year." (Don't ask me what year. I'm bad at math.) Emo Phillips made this joke famous, but most jokes cannot be traced back to a single inventor.

A man stands up at a prayer meeting and says: "Brothers and sisters, I have a wonderful testimony to divine providence to tell you about tonight. As I was walking to church half an hour ago I prayed to God that He would let me do some really good deed for Him, and He answered me instantly because I saw a man on a bridge about to jump off into the river. I ran up to him and said, 'Brother, don't do it!'

'Why not?' he said.

'Because your life is valuable.'

'Why?'

'Because God made you. Don't you believe in God? Are you an atheist?'

'No.'

'So you believe in God, then.'

'Yeah, I guess so.'

'What God? Are you a Christian, or a Muslim, or a Jew, or a Hindu, or what?'

'I'm a Christian.'

'So am I. See? Our God sent me to you tonight. He's our Father, and you're my brother.'

'Oh, I don't know about that.'

'You are my brother if you're a Christian. What kind of a Christian are you? Protestant or Catholic?'

'I'm a Protestant.'

'So am I. See? Our God sent me to you, brother.'

'I don't know, it may be just a coincidence.'

'What denomination are you?'

'I'm a Baptist.'

'So am I. See?' That proves it. You are my brother and our God sent me to you.'

'Well, maybe.'

'Tell me, are you a Northern Baptist or a Southern Baptist?'

'I'm a Southern Baptist.'

'So am I. See, you are my brother indeed, and our God sent me to save you. It's divine providence.'

'Well, I guess it's beginning to look like that.'

'Are you a Southern Baptist of the 1920 synod or a Southern Baptist of the 1930 synod?'

'I'm a Southern Baptist of the 1930 synod.'

So I said, 'Die, heretic!' and I pushed him off the bridge."

A similar, but more mercifully short joke:

A tourist was walking alone at night in Belfast during the "troubles" in Northern Ireland. Suddenly he felt strong arms around his body and a knife against his throat, and he heard a hoarse voice: "Tell me and tell me quick: are ye a Catlick or are ye a Proddystant?" The tourist thought: I have only a 50% chance to live unless I'm really clever. So he said, "I'm an atheist." The knife did not move. The voice demanded: "Catlick atheist or a Proddystant atheist?"

Now who's laughing at whom in these two jokes? Are Southern Baptists laughing at themselves in Emo Phillips' joke, or is everyone else laughing at Southern Baptists? Both! The joke is on both sides. Most good jokes are not one-sided and ideological, like propaganda or sneers, but are deliberately ambivalent in their point of view. The same is true of the Belfast joke: Protestants, Catholics, and atheists laugh at it equally, even though their points of view are opposite. It seems that humor overcomes this opposition as nothing else can, except perhaps life-or-death emergencies.

Humor does not by itself make us morally good and virtuous, but it helps. Aristotle ranked wit as one of the virtues. Wit is not just cleverness—that can be used for evil as well as good—but delight in a kind of play in words. If your life does not contain delight and play, you are missing a large dimension of moral goodness. Goodness is not merely duty; and we all know that instinctively and common-sensically—except the Stoics and rationalistic philosophers like Kant.

6. Humor and Beauty

Beauty is hard to define, but not hard to identify. We identify it by its effects. What is beautiful attracts us and makes us happy. It gives us joy. And the greatest joys provoke laughter, like Sam's joy at the end of *The Lord of the Rings*. So there is a natural connection between beauty and laughter, as between joy and laughter.

We experience joy whenever we discover or see beauty, and whenever we create beauty. The two most beautiful things we know are truth and goodness, light and love. Beauty is the child of truth and goodness, which are made for each other like men and women.

The beauty we see and enjoy and laugh at with the laughter of delight is objective; it is in the object, not only in the subject. True, "beauty is in the eye of the beholder," but it is not there alone. It is first of all in the eye of the beholdee. Dante found Beatrice's eyes far more beautiful than his own. But there is beauty also in Dante's right reaction to Beatrice's beauty. Both objective beauty and subjective beauty are occasions for the laughter of joy and delight.

The laughter of delight requires a childlike innocence. (Child-likeness is not the same as childishness. Saints are childlike; tyrants are childish.) That is why we find it in the Middle Ages more than in modern times, and among poor and "primitive" cultures like Africa more than among rich and sophisticated cultures like Western Europe. The Middle Ages were relatively simple and childlike and "primitive." This is a vice rather than a virtue in science and technology, but it is a virtue in art. The medievals were "primitive" in their technology in a negative way, but they were "primitive" in their art in a positive way, especially in their religious art. It is we moderns who are the artistic primitives and barbarians in a negative way. Our envious attempt to depict the "primitive" in art tends to brutalism and barbarism. It is childish rather than childlike, like a teenager acting like an infant with a tantrum.

The highest beauty is the beauty of wisdom and virtue, knowledge and love, truth and goodness. Like all beauty, this is both subjective ("in the eye of the beholder") and objective; both in our appreciation of truth or goodness and also in the truth or goodness itself. Like beauty, truth is also both objective and subjective: in the thing we know and in the minds that know it. And so is goodness: it is good to subjectively approve the objective good, and the objective good is what elicits the subjective good of love, appreciation, and approval.

To laugh at ugly things instead of beautiful things is an evil. In fact it is a terrible pathology because it is a perversion of a wonderful thing: the union of beauty and goodness. These were so closely connected by the ancient Greeks that they had a single word that meant both: "to kalon," which means both "the good" and "the beautiful." That unity is even laid out explicitly in the phrase "to kalon kai to agathon," "the beautiful and the good."

There are some beautiful things that are not good for us in our present disordered condition (e.g., Salome's dancing, which inspired Herod's lust and cost John the Baptist his head: Mark 6: 14-29). Even the beauty of the Face of God would probably overwhelm us and kill us in our present condition. (See Ex 33:20.) But there is nothing good that is not also beautiful. In abstract terms, beauty is always a property of goodness, although goodness (for us) is not always a property of beauty.

The Bible commands us to "rejoice (and, at its deepest, to laugh) with those who rejoice and to weep with those who weep." (Rom 12:15) Two terrible pathologies would be (1) to laugh and rejoice at those who weep (sneering scorn, or at least "Schadenfreude," taking joy in others' sufferings) and (2) to weep at those who laugh (envy, the only sin that never causes anyone any joy).

The Bible tells us that "there is a time to weep and a time to laugh" (Eccl 3:4); and therefore we are also told, insofar as we are sinners, to "mourn and weep; let your laughter be turned into mourning and your joy to dejection" (Jas 4:9). God habitually turns us upside-down people right side up by exalting the humble and humbling the exalted (Lk 14:11). Thus Jesus not only warns us that bad laughter turns to weeping ("woe to you that laugh now, for you shall mourn and weep"—Lk 6:25) but also promises us that good weeping turns to laughter ("Blessed are you that weep now, for you shall laugh"—Lk 6:21).

Which brings us to explore more deeply the relation between humor and suffering, or laughing and weeping.

7. Humor and Suffering

Suffering is not funny.

Ignorance is funny. Stupidity is funny. Impotence is funny. Clumsiness is funny. Ugliness is funny. Even sadness can be funny. But suffering is not funny, and neither is sin, especially the sin that causes suffering. Hitler's hysteria is funny, but his Holocaust is far from funny. Hell is not at all funny, though Heaven is, and perhaps even Purgatory.

Yet a strange kind of dark humor helped many of the Jews survive the Holocaust.

Sometimes suffering can be funny, to the sufferer, though not to the moral and compassionate observer. One of the best laughs I ever had in my life was when I was late for an important appointment (so terribly important that I completely forget what it was!) and I was driving through the dark and the rain and the fog and my tire blew. There was nothing to do but get out and change it, in my fancy clothes in the rain. As soon as I got out of the car, the rain doubled and the wind tripled. I got the car up on the jack and the jack collapsed. Just then, a big truck passed me and splattered my fancy clothes with not just rain but mud. It was so bad it was good; I broke out laughing hilariously.

But this was only a minor suffering. Minor tragedies can be comedies. Major tragedies cannot, at least in this life—though I strongly suspect that they may become hilariously funny in the next life.

Here is evidence that tragedy and comedy are not opposites. The sitcom episode voted the funniest ever was the "Chuckles the

Clown" episode on the old Mary Tyler Moore show. Mary and her friends on the news staff were at the funeral of their good friend Chuckles the circus clown, who had been trampled to death by an elephant. At the funeral parlor, Mary and her friends were at first terribly sad. But then they realized how ridiculously ironic and comic this death was for a clown, and this made it impossible *not* to want to laugh. They tried to suppress their giggles out of guilt. They failed, and finally let out their laughs uninhibitedly. And then they felt guilty, and sad again! —until someone said that that laughing of theirs was exactly what a good clown like Chuckles would have most wanted from them. And *that* made them cry more deeply than ever.

Here is another piece of evidence that tragedy and comedy are not opposites. Plato's masterpiece "The Symposium" ends with Socrates, having drunk all his friends under the table, debating the question whether comedy and tragedy are the same art or whether they are opposite arts. Anyone who understands Plato with the heart as well the head knows which of those options Socrates himself believes. Even Samuel Beckett, the nihilist existentialist atheist, entitled his masterpiece, "Waiting for Godot," "a tragicomedy," not "a tragedy." It is, in fact, my candidate for the funniest play ever written.

Humor contains an implicit philosophy of suffering: it whispers the secret that the tragicomedy of life is in the last analysis ultimately a comedy, not a tragedy; that, as Chesterton says, "the comedy of man survives the tragedy of man." Humor helps us to endure and even accept suffering, but it does not work the other way around. There can be an implicit, underground laughter hidden at the heart of suffering, but there is no implicit tragedy or suffering at the heart of genuine, hearty laughter, as opposed to bitter, cynical sarcasm. The heart of suffering points beyond itself to a final laughter; the heart of laughter does not point beyond itself to a final suffering.

Here are some examples of good jokes that fight against pain and misery, usually by making fun of our misery, or, rather, of our kvetching about it.

Four pessimists were arguing about which one's philosophy was the most pessimistic. The first said: "Blessed is he who dies as an infant before he see the sufferings of adult life." The second said: "And more blessed still is he dies in the womb and who never sees the light of day which exposes the fragility of all good things and leads only to death." The third said: "But most blessed of all is he who has not even been conceived." The fourth said: "Ah, yes, but how many of us have such good luck? Not one in a million."

A more serious joke about a more serious suffering:

During Stalin's reign of terror, two Jews were walking outside Moscow's Lubyanka prison, where thousands of their friends had been imprisoned, tortured, and killed. One, looking at the grim building, let out a long sigh. The other said, "Moishe, Moishe, how many times am I telling you not to make political statements in public?"

Humor is a weapon that enrages the tormentor and persecutor, because it reveals something—some reality or some point of view or some mode of consciousness or *something*—that transcends the tormentor's superior power and refuses to bow before it. That's one of the reasons why the Devil hates humor. (Another is that it makes us happy.)

There is a sense in which humor requires suffering: not merely in the sense that we appreciate things (like joy) best by contrast to their opposites (like suffering), but also in the sense that when we laugh at something funny we "suffer" not pain but joy. Thinking, desiring, attaning, willing, choosing, conquering, controlling— these are all activities. But suffering is a passivity, a reception, as the wax "suffers" the seal or the clay "suffers" the form of a pot to be imposed upon it. When we laugh we are not in control but in receptivity; not in the driver's seat but in the passenger's seat.

Why is this delightful? We may think it is because of the loss of responsibility that comes from being driven rather than driving; but that is not so, because what we receive from God is our human nature, which includes our free will and therefore our responsibility. Our very activity is received. Our free will is His grace, as His will is our peace. (Stop and think about that paradox!) This is delightful for a more positive reason: because it reveals a great truth, namely our ultimate ontological status: we are God's objects, God's gifts. This realization prompts gratitude. We are always receiving some grace from God, first of all our very existence. "Everything is a grace!" exclaimed St. Theresa on her deathbed.

But grace does not turn nature off but on. Receptivity to divine grace always results in more human activity, not less. At the beginning, what we *receive* by God creating us is *our own act* of existence. That first act (existence, actually) produces second acts (activities, operations). We act (and so does everything in the universe, in some way) because we are made by the God who is Pure Act. This is true in us in a higher way than in the rest of creation, which does not have free will, as we do; but we have free will only because we are predestined to have free will. Divine grace turns our freedom on, not off. The same is true in the intellect: we receive by faith truths from God that perfect our active reason. The same is true about the relation between our souls and our bodies: our active souls make our passive bodies, which are our souls' instruments, into responsible and active agents. And the principle also works for humor: our being the receptive butt of God's creative sense of humor creates our own art of creative humor.

8. Humor and Time

We can't be laughing all the time. Not being able to mourn is as much a fault as not being able to laugh. Ecclesiastes (3:4) says there is "a time to weep and a time to laugh, a time to mourn and a time to dance."

The Devil agrees with that verse, but his clocks run backwards. For him, the time to laugh is Good Friday and the time to mourn is Easter Sunday. Easter is the beginning of his Lent, not the end.

There is a time to fast and a time to feast. Fulton Sheen says there are two practical philosophies of life. The philosophy of the fool says: first the feast, then the fast. The philosophy of the wise says: first the fast, then the feast.

If you first play, then work, your play will be ruined by worry and your work will be ruined by hurry. For while you play you will worry that you will soon have to work, and while you work you will worry that you do not have enough time left to finish your work, so you will have to hurry because your play didn't leave enough time for work. Your play is ruined because you can't look forward with anticipation to your dreaded work, and your work is ruined because you can't look back on a job well done. You are upside down in time, doing the second thing first and the first thing second, just as you were upside down in space when the joke turned you right side up.

If you are that fool, you want your paycheck before you do your work, your feast before your fast, and your laughs before your tears. That's the Devil's philosophy. It spoils everything, even time.

When weeping comes first, it enhances the laughing afterwards. The more you let yourself weep, the more you can let yourself laugh. Laughing is the paycheck for weeping first (ask any saint), and weeping is the paycheck for laughing first (ask any convict).

The weeping that comes first does not last, because it is not last, it is not the last thing. Laughter ends it, and laughter lasts forever. For the fool, laughter comes first and does not last because it is not the last thing. Weeping ends it, and the weeping lasts forever. And that weeping is the only thing that is not funny in any way.

Furthermore, weeping is essentially temporal, temporary, a process. Weeping may be unending in Hell, but it is not eternal. Eternity is not unending time; it transcends time. Laughter, however, and the joy that prompts it, is made for eternity and fits eternity. Pleasure, comfort, satisfaction, and even happiness can be threatened by boredom because they are temporal, but joy cannot because it is timeless.

The only thing in this life that cannot be threatened by boredom is the love that is the gift of self. If the self is not given away, the self will eventually be bored. You may think that at least a few of the pleasures of this world might please you forever without boring you, but that is a delusion, and experience eventually confirms that. But the self-giving and self-forgetful love that gives itself away, that transcends itself, is not boring even in this temporal life. And the reason is that it does not come from this life or this world but into it from without, from the very life of God.

And since that life is beauty as well as truth and goodness, there is eternal joy and laughter as well as eternal wisdom and contemplation and eternal goodness and love. As beauty is the child of the marriage between truth and goodness, so eternal joy is the child of the marriage between eternal contemplation and eternal love.

Nothing else is infinite. Nothing else is absolute. Nothing else is eternal. Everything else gets boring.

Most knowledge, however true and good and necessary and useful, is not eternal wisdom, and thus not enough for a Heaven without boredom forever. Heaven is not simply an endless classroom or laboratory or library.

Most acts of charity, however virtuous, are not eternal, and thus not enough for a Heaven without boredom forever. Heaven is not simply an endless round of virtuous acts, public and private.

Most beautiful things and most beautiful words and most beautiful jokes are not eternal, and thus not enough for a Heaven without boredom forever.

But one is. That is God Himself. His infinity is not merely endless progress but timeless Allness. And we temporal creatures are invited to leap into that "consuming fire" that "eye has not seen, ear has not heard, nor has it entered into the heart of man." That is the Good News of "theosis." And that is the most delightfully funny joke ever told, by the Author and Master Comedian.

9. Humor and Jesus

Fr. Paul Murray, O.P. said in *Light at the Torn Horizon*, that "Humore will save the world."

Isn't that an exaggeration? No, for what God did in Christ to save us is the greatest of all tragedies in the services of the greatest of all comedies. The Cross is both the most horrific evil and suffering that ever happened *and* the greatest joke ever told, the one God played on the Devil.

All who go to Hell, like the Devil, have no sense of humor. They cannot let go of their sins and laugh at their own stupidity and ridiculousness; they cannot go along with God's great joke. They are scandalized by God's laughter. Salvation and simple seriousness are mutually exclusive.

Chesterton's insight, at the very end of his masterpiece *Orthodoxy*, that Jesus may have concealed his humor because it was too much for us to endure, surprises us because it is so rarely said. But his sense of humor is pervasive, and if we miss it, we miss a dimension of his human nature that is not accidental. We probably suspect that dimension because we think humor contradicts seriousness, and salvation from sin and death and Hell is the most serious business in the world. And it is! But that means not that the savior is the man with the least sense of humor but the man with the greatest. Because all the best jokes are about the most serious things: religion, politics, sex, suffering, and stupidity. Jesus proves that our assumption that humor contradicts or detracts from seriousness is a false one.

Take a typical concrete example. John's Gospel is the profoundest and the most serious, so it ought to be also the most humorous. Take a typical chapter, chapter 5. I have found five points in this chapter that sent me into hysterical laughter when I "got the point," and I'm sure there must be even more.

(1) First, the problem Jesus addresses there is itself funny in a Monty Python sort of way. It's a "catch-22.":

"Now there is in Jerusalem by the Sheep Gate a pool, in Hebrew called Bethsatha (or Bethesda or Bethsaida), which has five porticoes."

(By the way, God played a small joke on the skeptical scholars of Biblical history here. Five was not a sacred number to the Jews, so the skeptics said this incident could not have really happened in Jerusalem and must have been a story imported from a Gentile author, because no architectural feature in all of Jewish history has a significant "five" in it. And then archeologists in the 20th century actually found that pool with the five porticoes, right where John said it was.)

"In these (porticoes) lay a multitude of invalids, blind, lame, paralyzed, waiting for the moving of the water; for an angel of the Lord went down at certain seasons into the pool and troubled the water; whoever stepped in first after the troubling of the water was healed of whatever disease he had. One man was there who had been ill for thirty-eight years. When Jesus saw him and knew that he had been lying there a long time, he said to him, 'Do you want to be healed?'"

There is almost a joke here too, by the way. Imagine this poor sucker, lame for 38 years, putting all his hopes for a cure in this pool, probably camped out by it every day of his life. Asking him if he wants to be cured is like asking Charlie Brown whether he'd like to actually kick Lucy's football this time, or asking someone in Hell whether he'd rather be in Heaven. For the sign on the door of Hell that reads "Abandon all hope, ye who enter here" on the outside reads "No Exit" on the inside.

"The sick man answered him, 'Sir, I have no man to put me into the pool when the water is troubled, and while I am going another steps down before me."

55

Why does he need so desperately to get into that water? Because he is crippled. Why can't he ever get into that water? Because he is crippled. Catch-22.

Imagine the Monty Python characters doing this skit in their inimitably English tone of voice, a cheery fatalism that is funny because it's self-contradictory—like Monty Python's satire on pop psychology in "The Life of Brian" where Jesus teaches the two dying thieves to sing "Silver Lining" as they hang there. (No, that's not blasphemous; it's a satire on pop psychology, not on Christianity.) My friend actually heard a homily by a pop-psychologist priest in the 60's saying that the message Jesus tried to get across to humanity from His pulpit on the Cross was: "I'm OK, you're OK." The appalling and the hilarious can often coincide.

(2) And then comes the solution, which is even funnier than the problem:

"Jesus said to him, 'Rise, take up your pallet, and walk.' And at once the man was healed, and he took up his pallet and walked." Jesus cuts through the rules of the game and the angel who is the middleman (they're his angels, after all!) in the same way Harrison Ford cuts through the rules of combat by whip and sword in "Indiana Jones and the Temple of Doom": with a cynical "oh, the Hell with it" look, he pulls his gun out and *shoots* the big guy with the whip. It's like Alexander the Great "solving" the problem of "untying" the Gordian knot with a single cut of his sword. Everyone who saw that must have thought, "Hey, why didn't we think of that?" The answer was that they were in a joke and they were the "straight men."

(3) And then the idiotic Pharisees prove to be even funnier than the straight men by their crookedness:

"Now that day was the Sabbath. So the Jews said to the man who was cured, "It is the Sabbath, it is not lawful for you to carry your pallet."

In other words, "Sorry, you're not allowed to be cured today. It's the 'no-walking' day. Get back in bed."

What's that like? It's like the friends of a man who got a heart transplant complaining that the heart he got was in a box that was labeled "Do not open until Christmas." It's like a policeman's colleagues complaining that he was speeding when he caught the criminal. It's like Juliet's friend complaining that Romeo's love letter had a grammatical mistake in it.

(4) And then comes Jesus's reaction to this idiocy, when they accuse the doctor of doing his job:

"And this was why the Jews persecuted Jesus, because he did this on the Sabbath. But he answered them, "My Father is working still, and I am working."

If His Father had stopped working, they and they whole world would have disappeared into nothingness, because everything that is made tends to fall back into that out of which it was made unless maintained in existence (e.g., brown wood painted white turns back to brown unless repainted), and that out of which God made the universe was nothing. When God stops working, so do we! So their complaint was implicitly a complaint against their own existence.

So either we are not yet in the seventh day, the day of God's rest, and the end of time; or else God is still working today, on the seventh day, not to create but to preserve and heal. Jesus manifests the Father, and Jesus works, therefore the Father works. Like Father, like Son.

(5) And then Jesus adds one more "zinger" to his critics:

"You search the Scriptures because you think that in them you have eternal life; and it is they that bear witness to me; yet you refuse to come to me that you may have life."

Imagine Juliet knocking on Romeo's door: "Romeo, Romeo, where are you?" And Romeo replies: "Go away, I'm busy." "What are you doing?" "I'm mooning at my photo album full of pictures of my beloved Juliet."

That's essentially the same joke as the one about the theologian who died and was given the choice by God between going to Heaven or going to a theology lecture about Heaven, and he chose the lecture.

Appendix: My Favorite Jokes

The existence of this Appendix will prevent some serious readers from taking this book seriously. After all, it is little more than a re-telling of the jokes that have made me laugh the most and that have, in my experience, also made others laugh the most.

That is not a very difficult or original thing to do; almost any-one could do it. In contrast, philosophizing about humor is much more rare, since not many people classify themselves as philoso-phers, and of those who do, very few write about humor, while most people can and do tell jokes.

Yet I think I have done more of a good service to my readers in this Appendix than in the book proper, because they will prob-ably enjoy it more and certainly remember it better.

A Defense of Jokes

Jokes are invented by human beings, of course, but their in-ventors are anonymous, like the builders of the Gothic cathe-drals. They are not copyrighted. They circulate by human speech before they are written down in books, and the authors of those books are never sued for plagiarism. Jokes, like sun-beams, are common property. They are one of the few things in life that don't ever make lawyers rich. How much money do jokes make? As much as the yearly Gross National Product of Utopia.

Jokes need a defense today, because they are not sophisticated, scientific, or scholarly. They are "populist."

Jokes are very short stories. Stories are humanity's earliest and commonest art form. The only rivals to stories for the most universal and primitive art is the funerary arts. But death, which seems to be totally un-funny, has inspired some of the funniest jokes of all. Humor and death seem to go together, as if Heaven, which invented life, is laughing at Hell's invention of death.

Jokes and parables are both short stories. If you don't classify Jesus's favorite literary form as inferior, why do you class a similar literary form as inferior if its point is not to teach a moral lesson but to make you laugh? And quite often, jokes do both.

Jokes are tiny stories that tell larger stories, parts of life that concretize and exemplify and symbolize something about life as a whole. So are parables. What's the difference between parables and jokes, then? The point of a parable is usually moral or practical. Parables tell us what ought to be, in contrast to what is. That is why we need morality: because of that contrast. The point of jokes is more theoretical, that is, contemplative. Jokes show us what is, often in contrast to what ought to be. And that is why we need humor too, because of that same contrast.

All of life has a moral dimension; that is why there are parables. And all of life is funny; that's why there are jokes. Both are icons or symbols or myths: all of life is concentrated into a concrete little part of life to show that life is war, or life is love, or life is a surprise, or life is a bowl of cherries, or life is a game, or life is a work of art, or life is Alice's Restaurant. That is also what myths are. Jokes are little myths. They have a point, and it is always possible to myth the point.

Not all humor comes in the form of jokes, of course. But much of it does. Jokes are to humor what syllogisms are to arguments. Some philosophers (Hobbes, e.g.) are fanatically allergic to syllogisms. That's like being allergic to odd numbers, which is as odd as being allergic to odd stories. Jokes are odd stories. Allergies to oddities are odder than otters. It's almost a kind of idiocy, so

HA!

that we could call it Homeric and speak of the Idiot and the Odd-ity, if we had appundicitis.

So here are some of my favorite jokes that I could not integrate into my pseudo-philosophical text.

I reluctantly classify them into religious jokes, political jokes, lawyer jokes, Jewish jokes, Irish jokes, etc. I do it reluctantly because life does not throw humor at us in classified forms. I classify them only to give the book the deceptive look of being serious and philosophical enough to be publishable. The deception worked: it fooled at least one publisher.

Why is there no section on sexual jokes? For in the "real world" those are probably the single most pervasive kind of jokes. My answer is not because of some Puritanical or Victorian prudery or because sex is somehow "dirty," but because sex is so beautiful and holy. It is the source of life itself. Therefore, although sex jokes are not usually consciously meant as sacrilegious or blasphemous, they often are in fact, or at least sail close to that edge. The two holiest places in the world are a woman's womb and a Catholic altar, because those are the two places where, throughout the world and millions of times every day, God performs literal miracles that have eternal consequences. In the womb, He changes matter into spirit, or nothingness into persons, by creating rational souls; and on the altar he changes bread and wine into the Body and Blood of the Second Person of the Holy Trinity.

That is why contraception is wrong: it is as sacrilegious or blasphemous as a priest saying Mass but deliberately faking rather than actually saying the words of consecration, "This Is My Body," in order to keep God away, because he does not want to receive the very greatest gift that God gives us. Contraceptives are padlocks on our door against The Intruder.

There are also no feminist jokes or racist (as distinct from racial) jokes here, because there are many people who are so super-sensitive to this dimension because of our sad history of sneering superiority

60

at the "other" gender or other races. Sneering is the very lowest form of humor, and higher forms of humor in these sensitive areas tend to be misunderstood and reduced to the lowest form.

But Blacks, Jews, and the Irish gleefully and healingly tell these jokes on themselves, and some are so funny that they can't be ignored. Perhaps some day feminists will also change their anger into humor.

Jewish Jokes

It is empirically evident that the Jews and the Irish tell the best jokes and produce the most comedians. Perhaps that is because they *are* the best jokes. Or perhaps they specialize in humor because they also specialize in suffering, historically. And the connection between suffering and humor is clearly not a coincidence. That also explains the Irish, who are the world's second best at both.

Jews cannot escape either history, their culture, their race, or their religion, no matter how hard they try. There are many good religious jokes, which are directed not at God or at holy things but at the jackasses God uses to carry Him into Jerusalem.

Many religious jokes, especially "priest, minister and rabbi jokes," are deliberately ambivalent in their perspective. For instance, here is a Jewish joke that can easily be misunderstood as either anti-Jewish or anti-Christian, though it is neither. And most people, both Jews and Christians, understand that it is neither because it makes both laugh. Which, incidentally, is an impressive piece of evidence for the power of laughter to do what careful and polite interfaith dialog often fails to do.

A Jewish couple comes to their rabbi looking distraught.
The rabbi asks what is the matter.
They reply:
"We once had a son, and now we think he is no longer our son."

The rabbi asks: "Why, what did he do?"

They answer: "He is dating a goi, a Christian."

"Oh!" says the rabbi. "I know how you feel."

"Do you really know how we feel, rabbi? Did that ever happen to you?"

"Not only that, but something worse than that. I too once had a son, and he not only dated a Christian but he married her."

"Oh, how awful! How did you cope? What did you do?"

"I did the same thing you did: I went to higher authority: to the Chief Rabbi."

"And what did he say to you?"

"He said the same thing to me as I am saying to you. He said: 'I know how you feel. I too once had a son, but it was even worse: he *became* a Christian.' So I asked him the same question you are asking me: 'How did you cope?' And he said: 'I did the same thing you did: I went to higher authority.' So I asked him: 'Higher authority? What higher authority is there than you?' And he said: 'I got an interview with the Almighty.' And I said: 'That's amazing. And what did the Almighty say?' And he said: 'The Almighty said to me: I know how you feel. I too once had a Son....'"

Jews love to laugh at themselves. For example:

An Orthodox Jewish congregation was bitterly divided about women's rights. The conservatives insisted on keeping the women segregated from the men at worship. They also insisted on not allowing women to be cantors. The revisionists argued that nothing in the Law prevented those two reforms.

The rabbi tried to make peace, but his congregation would not stop arguing angrily with each other. The leader of the conservative faction insisted that sex segregation was "the way we have always done it," from the beginning of their congregation a hundred years ago. The leader of the reformist faction insisted that that was not true, that "the way we have always done it" was that the congregation used to allow these reforms from the beginning.

Finally, the rabbi persuaded both faction leaders to accept the judgment of the only man who could remember how the congregation really did it from its beginning a century ago. That was a very old and wise rabbi who was 110 years old and in a nursing home.

So they all went to see him and explained the situation and asked for his judgment. The conservative leader insisted that his way was "the way they had always done it," but the old rabbi was not convinced. The reformist leader then made his case that his way was "the way they had always done it," but the old rabbi was not convinced. The two leaders then resumed their heated argument with each other in front of the old rabbi.

The old rabbi then responded, "Ah, yes, now *that* is the way we have always done it."

Here is another self-deprecating Jewish joke that can be misused by an anti-Semite:

A Jewish mother and her five-year-old son were swimming at Coney Island when a sudden rogue wave swallowed the boy and took him out to sea, apparently to his death. The mother loudly complained to God, shaking her fist at the heavens: "You can't have him! It's unjust! Give him back to me! I am his mother!" As if in response, the ocean immediately produced another giant wave which spit the boy out onto the beach uninjured. The mother looked over him carefully, then said to God: "He had a hat!"

Irish Jokes

The Irish love to talk, and that is their glory. There are probably more Irish jokes than any other kind, and inevitably most of them are going to be second-rate. That is my justification for confining myself to a very few. All of them are about the second great gift God gave us through the Irish, after their words, namely their whiskey.

Paddy McGillicuddy worked at the Guinness factory, and he loved it, because he loved Guinness. One working day the owner of the factory showed up at the door of his house. His wife opened the door. The owner looked very serious, and said,

"I'm afraid I have to deliver you some bad news, Mrs. McGillicuddy. Your husband just had an accident at the factory."

"Oh dear! That's bad news indeed. How bad is he?"

"Well, I think he's fine now. But that's because he's in Heaven. He's gone."

"Gone? The news gets even worse! What happened to him?"

"Well, he drowned."

"Drowned? We're nowhere near the sea."

"Well, he drowned in a big vat of Guinness."

"Oh dear! Worse and worse it gets. Well, at least I hope he went quick."

"Well, Mrs. McGillicuddy, I fear I have even more bad news for you. It took almost all morning."

"Worst of all! How did that happen so?"

"Well, he had to take three trips to the water closet."

Pat and Mike are best buddies. They're both getting long in the tooth, so Pat says one day to Mike, "Mike, ye are me best friend, are ye not?"

"Oh, that I am, Pat, that I am."

"I want ye to prove it to me."

"And how shall I do that, Pat?"

"Well, if I go first, I want ye to celebrate me."

"And how do ye want me to do that?"

"By buyin' the very best of the gold stuff."

"You mean Irish whiskey, right?"

"Right. The three hundred Euros a bottle stuff."

"Oh, Pat, I shall be happy to do that for ye, O me best buddy."

"Ah, but then I want ye to prove to the world the high regard ye hold me in by pouring it all on me grave."

At that Pat almost stops breathing. "A whole bottle of the gold stuff poured out on yer grave?"

"That's it. That will prove to the world how ye hold me in the very highest regard."

Pat is silent, thinking.

"Will ye do that for me, Mike?"

"Why sure I will, Pat, sure I will. But I trust ye will understand that I shall have to run it through me kidneys first."

Clancy owns a bar in Dublin and Brandon is his best customer. One day Brandon is the only one in the bar. Clancy is polishing classes in the rear. In comes a man who doesn't look Irish. He dresses funny, walks funny, talks funny. He sits down next to Brandon. Brandon strikes up a conversation. "Welcome, stranger. I'd guess ye are not from round here, am I right?"

"Yeah, that's right," the stranger says, in a thick New York accent.

"I'd be guessin' ye hail from the other side of the pond. Am I right?"

"Yup."

"And what brings ye to our fair isle, now?"

"Work."

"What kind of work?"

"Teaching. I'm teaching at the University for the spring term."

"Ah. So what do ye teach, then?"

"Logic."

"Logic! Here in Ireland? Ye won't get many students to show up for that."

"What do you mean?"

"Why, we don't need any logic. We're Irish. We don't believe in logic. We've got somethin' better than logic. We've got magic."

"Well, logic is a kind of magic. It has a kind of magical power. It's called deduction."

"What's that? Got something to do with ducks, has it?"

"No. If I use the power of deduction, I can bring to light hidden things, things that you might not want me to know. If you tell me one little thing, I can deduce many other things, greater things, hidden things."

"No ye can't. Not if I don't want you to know them. Give me a fer-instance."

"All right. I can use the power of deduction to reveal some of the secrets of your sex life from the contents of your garage."

"Nonsense. I'd like to see you try."

"Fine. Just tell me: do you have a lawnmower in your garage?"

"A lawnmower?"

"Yeah. You know what a lawnmower is, don't you?"

"Of course. What's that got to do with my sex life?"

"I'll show you. If you have a lawnmower, I deduce that you have a lawn."

"Well, of course I do. Why would I buy a lawnmower if I didn't have a lawn?"

"And I further deduce that if you have a lawn, you have a house."

"Well, that's so. Ye never saw me house. But lawns go with houses, there's no magic in that."

"And if you have a house, you probably have a family."

"Well, yes, 'tis true, 'tis true. Maybe there's something to this deduction after all. Here, I have pictures of me wife and me twelve kids here in me wallet. Would you like to see them?"

"No, I'd like to deduce again. And I deduce that if you have a family, you are a heterosexual."

"Omigosh! 'Tis magic indeed! The secrets of me sex life deduced from the contents of me garage! Tell me, Professor, can I learn to do this magic too, this dee-duction thing that you do?"

"Of course. Just come to my class at the university tomorrow morning."

"Oh, I will, I will. Thank you for sharing your magic powers with us."

The stranger exits, and Clancy appears. "Who was that strange fellow who dressed a little funny and walked a little funny and talked a little funny?"

"Oh, Clancy, he's a magician. That's what he is."

"Where's he from?"

"New York."

"There ain't no magic in New York. I know three fellas who moved there. There's dirt, and cops, and mugging, but there ain't no magic."

"Oh, but there is, and this fella brought some here. The magic is called dee—duck somethin' or other. And he teaches it. It's called Logic."

"Logic? You mean deduction? That's not magic."

"Oh, but it is, Clancy. It can reveal hidden secrets. Here, let me show you. If you tell me just one thing, I can deduce hidden things. In fact I can reveal the secrets of your sex life from the contents of your garage."

"Nonsense. You can't do that."

"I can, with this magic! Here, just tell me one thing, Clancy: do ye have a lawnmower in yer garage?"

"A lawnmower?"

"Yeah, a lawnmower. Ye know what that is, don't ya?"

"Of course."

"Well, have ye got one?"

"No, I don't. So what?"

"Clancy, Clancy, I bin comin' to yer bar for nigh onto thirty year now, and I thought I knew ye, but it takes this furriner's magic to bring ye out of the closet!"

(This joke is also actually a logic joke. What we are laughing at is actually Brandon's implied fallacy of an illicit major in the enthymeme: All who have lawnmowers in their garage are heterosexuals, and Clancy does not have a lawnmower in his garage, therefore Clancy is not a heterosexual.)

Religious Jokes

Jokes, like conversation, have two sides or two poles: the one outside the joke who tells the joke and the ones inside the joke who are the butt of the joke. Religion also has two sides or two poles: God and Man. The very word "religion" comes from the Latin "religare" or "religio," which means "relationship," or "binding relationship," or "binding-back relationship." It is not healthy, holy, or safe to laugh at God's pole in that relationship, but it is very healthy and even holy to laugh at ourselves. In fact it is unhealthy not to.

Religion is both the funniest and most serious thing in human life. It generates the most passion, both for good and for evil, and it makes the most astonishing and apparently outrageous claims. Yet it at least makes life more interesting and passionate than anything else does. People will die for it, and also kill for it, throughout history. And it is the single most adamantly affirmed and valued thing in life, at least for most human beings throughout history and in all cultures except one (our own). And even here, although it's passe in Harvard and Hollywood, it's still pretty robust for most of the people in most of the flyover places between the two H's.

Religious jokes are probably more interesting, more sought-out, and more told by religious people than by non-religious people, but both classes of people find them funny, often for opposite reasons: each side thinks it's laughing at the other side and yet at the same time secretly wonders whether it isn't also laughing at itself. If religion divides us more than anything else, this secret sameness seems to speak of something more mysterious that unites us even in the thing that divides us.

Among Catholics, the Jesuits tell the most jokes—of course mainly on themselves. For instance:

What is the difference between a Jesuit and a Dominican?

The Dominicans were founded by St. Dominic in the 12th century to combat the heresy of Albigensianism. The Jesuits were founded by St. Ignatius Loyola in the 16th century to combat the heresy of Protestantism. Now tell me, how many Albigensians have you met lately?

It is significant that both Jesuits and Dominicans tell that one. As they do the next one:

A Catholic layman goes to confession to his priest. He says, "Father, I confess an ongoing sin of lust. But it's not sexual. It's automotive."

"What do you mean?"

"I lust for a Lexus. I just have to have one."

"Well, it's not a sin to have one."

"Oh, but I can't afford one."

"So what are you doing about that?"

"Well, I figure the only way I can scrape together enough money to buy one is by winning the lottery. But there's not much chance of that unless I get supernatural help. Now I have a great devotion to the Blessed Virgin Mary, so I want to say a novena to her for the Lexus. But I feel that that's probably sacrilegious. Tell me, Father: Is it sacrilegious to say a novena for a Lexus?"

"Hmmm. You know, they never taught us about that in seminary. I'll tell you what to do. There's a very holy priest in the next parish, a Franciscan. If anybody knows the answer to your question, he does. Go ask him."

So the man goes to the Franciscan holy man, tells his story, and then asks his question: "So tell me, Father, is it sacrilegious to say a novena for a Lexus?"

And the priest asks, "A Lexus? What is a Lexus?"

The man thinks: "This guy is living in another world. He can't understand my obsession. I'll go to a Jesuit. They're more worldly. He'll understand."

So he goes to a Jesuit and tells his story and asks his question: "So is it sacrilegious to say a novena for a Lexus?"

And the Jesuit replies: "A novena? What is a novena?"

Guess what religious group tells the following one:

A Jewish couple comes to their rabbi and says: "We are worried about our son. We want him to be either a rabbi or a lawyer, but we think he is going to be an alcoholic. Is there any way we can know his future?"

The rabbi replies: "Does he live with you?"

"Yes."

"What is the first thing he sees when he comes in your house?"

"The table inside the front door."

"Then I suggest a scientific experiment. Put a Bible and a bottle of booze and a wad of bills on the table and watch which one he picks up first. If it's the Bible, he will become a rabbi. If it's the booze, he will become an alcoholic. If it's the bills, he will become a lawyer."

So the couple goes home to do their little experiment, and the next time they meet the rabbi he asks: "Did you do what I suggested?"

"Yes, we did."

"And what was the result?"

"Well, he picked up all three together and hugged them close to his heart. What does that mean?"

"Oy vey, I have some very bad news for you. Your son, he is going to become a Jesuit."

A monk asked his abbot if it was permissible to smoke while he prayed, and the abbot said No. Seeing another monk smoking while praying, the monk said, "Did you ask the abbot for permission to do that?"

The second monk said, "Yes, I did."

"And the abbot told you it was OK?"

"Yes."

"How did you get that answer? What did you say to him?"

"I just asked him if it was permissible to pray while I smoked."

There are fewer Protestant jokes than Catholic jokes, probably because protesting (which is by definition what Protestants are: protesters) is never as funny as the thing being protested against.

There is, of course, the famous Puritan (or Dutch Calvinist) joke:

Why are Puritans (or Calvinists) forbidden to make love standing up? Because it might lead to dancing.

Here's a Protestant joke that depends on terminology, on the Protestant substitute for "Mass" or "Sacred Liturgy":

Little Johnny took everything literally, so when he heard his parents worrying about him and saying, "What can we do with Johnny? He's bored to death in church," he started worrying too.

The following Sunday, after the morning church service, Johnny asked the preacher about the names on a big brass headstone in the churchyard. The preacher said, "Oh, those are the names of all our parishioners who died in the service."

Johnny nodded knowingly, and asked, "Was it the morning service or the evening service?"

Another Protestant joke (which is also a Catholic joke), from another, earlier and simpler time:

The Bishop was visiting a fifth-grade class at a Catholic girl's school, and asked each of the girls what she wanted to be when she grew up.

One of the girls said she wanted to whisper her answer in his ear, and he nodded agreement. But when she whispered her answer, the bishop fainted dead away.

When he recovered, the teacher asked the girl what she said that had made the Bishop faint. The girl confessed that she had said that she wanted to be a prostitute.

The Bishop heard this, apologized for fainting, and said to her, "Oh, I'm sorry, my dear. My hearing is getting bad. I thought I heard you say you wanted to be a Protestant."

Here is a generic religious joke:

A pious little old lady and an atheist live right next to each other. Every day the little old lady went out her door and prayed aloud, "Thank you, Lord, for another day." The atheist would hear her and shout back, "There is no God!" This happened every day.

One day the little old lady ran into serious money problems, and when she went out her door she prayed a different prayer: "Thank you, Lord, for another day, and thank you for what I know you will do for me: thank you for providing for me the groceries I can't afford any more."

The atheist heard her and says, "There is no God to buy your groceries for you, stupid!"

The next morning, the lady found a bag of groceries on her front step, and she prayed, "Thank you, Lord, for providing for me."

The atheist, who was listening, jumped out of his hiding place and said, "Gotcha! *I* bought you those groceries, not God."

The lady replied, "Thank you, Lord, for not only providing my groceries for me but also for making Satan pay for them."

Here is a generic religious riddle: what is a dyslexic insomniac agnostic?

Answer: Someone who stays up all night wondering: Is there a DOG?

Religious role reversal sometimes works paradoxically in jokes. Here is the atheist Carl Sagan's answer to how to make an apple pie from scratch:

"First, create a universe…"

Jokes about religion and political correctness can be double-barreled funny. Like the one about the pronoun wars at the very politically correct Harvard Divinity School:

The feminists refused to use the traditional pronoun for God, "He," because they said it meant that God is male, and "if God is male, then male is God." (Forget the logical fallacy of the illicit conversion of a universal affirmative proposition there, just play along.)

So the authorities changed the pronoun for God to "he or she."

But the feminists still complained that "he" came first, so women were still second-class citizens.

So in reparation of traditional male chauvinism they changed the God pronoun to "she or he."

But then the wiccans and the Gaia people and the earth-first people and the tree-huggers complained that they had forgotten the divinity of the planet.

So they added "it." So now the politically-correct pronoun for God was "she or he or it."

But that took too long to say, so they decided to condense it to one syllable.

(NB please remember that the object of this joke is Harvard feminists, not God. Certainly not the God who "sitteth in the heavens (and) shall laugh.")

A philosophy professor died and found himself outside the gates of Heaven. God came out to meet him and said, "Welcome. We've been expecting you." Then God pointed to a group of red brick buildings in the distance and said, "That's where you go."

"What is that?" asked the philosopher.

"It's Harvard University."

"Oh. What is it doing here?"

"Well, you see, in this place everyone gets what they love the most, so everyone one who loves wisdom the most goes to Heaven and everyone who loves philosophy the most goes to Harvard."

"But I'm a philosopher, and philosophy is the love of wisdom, so I should go to Heaven."

"No, you're not a philosopher, you're a philosophy *professor.* You only profess to be a philosopher."

Two men die at the same time and go to Heaven. When St. Peter opens the golden gates, he says to them, "The first rule here is never to step on a duck."

They look around them and there are ducks everywhere. They try to avoid stepping on them, but the first man accidentally steps on one, and its quack of protest brings St. Peter with a set of chains and a very ugly woman.

"You violated the first rule, so your Purgatory will be to be chained to this woman for a hundred years."

The second man sees this and is extremely careful not to step on a duck, and succeeds, for a long time. Eventually St. Peter comes to him with another chain and another woman, but this woman is totally gorgeous.

St. Peter chains the man and the woman together and says, "That's 100 years for you two."

The man says to the woman, "I wonder what we did to deserve that?"

The woman replies, "I don't know what you did, but all I did was to step on a duck."

The very best religious joke of all time is not one in words. It is that God loves us. Us! The beautiful princess loves *frogs*, and goes around the world kissing them and turning them into princes.

Computer Jokes

Computers have no sense of humor. That's the only thing that's funny about them. That's one of the ways they resemble Hitler.

Another way is that they are shameless liars. I just lost all the computer jokes I put into this computer by clicking "save" and trusting my little liar. (That's not a joke; that's a fact.)

I've asked dozens of people I've met who are in the computer industry whether they have ever heard of the following event having actually happened at any time or place in the history of the world: someone clicked on the "help" icon and actually got help. They all smiled and said No. Computers never smile. But they are very good at saying No.

The first famous computer joke, in the high holy heyday of the early computer revolution, was about the great supercomputer which was designed to answer every possible question. The first question its designers asked it was: "Is there a God?" It answered: "There is *now!*"

Two pilots in a helicopter were lost in a dense fog. They had lost all their instruments and they had only five minutes of fuel left.

The pilot said, "I have no idea where we are. But I see some tall buildings below poking up through the fog, so I'm going to fly down there and ask for directions."

He circled the building and saw a man in the top floor window. The pilot yelled out the window, "Where the hell are we?" but the man in the window couldn't hear him.

"Quick," said the pilot to the copilot, "Is there a big magic marker and a posterboard in the cabin?"

"Yes, here they are."

"Good. Write in big letters 'WHERE THE HELL ARE WE?' and hang it out the window as I circle that building again.

They did it, and the man made a big circle with his arm. The pilot said, "He understands, and he's asking us to circle around again for the answer." But they had only two minutes of fuel left.

When they circled the building again, the man was holding a big white posterboard out the window with the answer written with his magic marker. It read: "YOU ARE IN A HELICOPTER."

The copilot started cursing out the man, but the pilot simply smiled, sent the helicopter off at just the right angle, and landed on the landing field just as the fuel ran out.

"That was a miracle!" he said to the pilot. "How did you do that?"

"Well," said the pilot, "when I saw the tall buildings, I knew we were over either Vancouver or Seattle or Portland. And when I saw the man's answer I knew exactly where we were: that's Bill Gates's Microsoft building. I recognized his definition of 'user friendly.'"

Puns

Those who do not love puns usually do not love language, or at least do not love language's wonderful elasticity and ambiguity. Everything in the universe, except for numbers, is a pun of some sort because all words are either equivocal or analogical.

A scientist successfully cloned a human being, and wanted to present his achievement to his peers at a scientific meeting in an auditorium in the penthouse on the 50th story of a city skyscraper. But the clone had Tourette's Syndrome, and frequently uttered a string of obscenities. So before showing his clone to the audience, the scientist warned him, "If you say your usual obscenities while you are on stage, I will kill you. I made you, I can unmake you just as easily." But the clone replied by spouting a horrible streak of obscenities. So the scientist made good on his threat and took his clone out onto the balcony of the penthouse of the fifty story building and throw him to the ground, where he broke into pieces. But when the police came by to arrest him, the scientist could only be charged with making an obscene clone fall.

Little Sammy loved his teddy bear, so it surprised his parents when he rearranged the bear's eyes so that the pupils were no longer in the center of the cornea looking ahead, but were looking at each other cross-eyed. And then Sammy named the bear "Gladly." They asked him why he did that, and he said "I wanted him to be the bear we sing about in church in that hymn, you know, "Gladly the cross I'd bear."

Rudolph and his wife Olga lived in a cabin in northern Russia. One day, in the middle of winter, it got warm enough to rain instead of snow. Rudolph said to Olga, "Olga! Come look, my dear, it's raining." Olga replied, "Impossible. You are mistaken." Rudolph replied, "Not so! Rudolph the Red knows rain dear."

The two bassists in the string section of the New York Philharmonic symphony orchestra were both Irish, and both loved their Guinness. They were playing the last movement of Beethoven's Ninth Symphony when suddenly the conductor stopped conducting and struggled with the pages of the score, because when he tried to turn the page, he found that the next few pages would not open because they were tied together with strong string and many knots. The orchestra had to stop the performance until this was corrected. At this point, bassist #1 whispered to bassist #2: "I did that. It will take exactly twenty minutes to untie those knots. We can slip out and have a Guinness at Clancy's bar right across the street—no one will notice because we're in the back row—and we can be back before the music begins again." So they left their bass fiddles and snuck out to Clancy's. They gulped down no less than four pints in twenty minutes. When they returned, drunk, they found that the pages of the score were still tied together and the conductor was still struggling, but that Mariano Rivera, the New York Yankees' great relief pitcher, had been called onto the stage. They asked the others in the orchestra why he was there, and the reply was: "Well, it's the last of the ninth and the score is tied and the bassists are loaded."

There is literally a little town in New Jersey that is the only town in the world whose name is the answer to the question, How can a naked man who just drank six beers escape being eaten by a hungry lion? Its name is Piscataway.

Here is the backstory of the beheading of John the Baptist. The reason King Herod was so smitten with Salome the dancing girl when she danced for him was because she was Italian and therefore very beautiful. She had lived with her mother in Genoa, Italy, where they ran a little Italian deli before they moved to Israel even though the food was not as good. When lustful Herod made his foolish promise to Salome to give her anything up to half his kingdom, she asked her mother what she should ask for, and her mother said, "The head of John the Baptist." The promise was made publicly, so Herod had to fulfill his promise. But the executioner was sick, so Herod's provost had to do the job in his place. He was a good friend of Herod's (Herod called him simply "Prov") and he was a jack of all trades, but he warned Herod that the execution would be difficult because John had a very hard head and a very stiff neck. Herod replied, "When the king orders beheadings, heads will roll!" The Provost replied, "I'll do my best, but to make this guy's head roll is going to be hard." Salome's mother wanted to come and watch the execution with Salome and the provost but Salome said, "Mother, you can't come with me." "Why not?" her mother asked. "Because of what you taught us back when we ran that Italian deli: Genoa salami goes with provolone on a hard roll."

Riddles

These are even more childish than puns, but there is a time to be childish and a time to be a dolt.

Four people walk down the street: Santa Claus, Jesus, the Tooth Fairy, and an honest lawyer. They all see a $1000 bill on the street. Which one would pick it up and put it in his pocket?
Jesus. The other three are myths.

Stupid riddle: What word do all New Yorkers pronounce wrong? Answer: "Wrong."

Even stupider riddle: What's pink, six feet long, shaped like a banana, flies, and whistles? Answer: a pink, six-foot long flying, whistling banana.

One-Liners

If jokes are short stories, one liners are very short stories.

Emo Phillips' one-liner, beloved of all kids: "My dear, your evening gown is adorable. You look so *slinky* there at the top of the stairs."

Stephen Wright's puzzlingly philosophical one-liner: "I came home and found that every single thing I owned had been stolen and replaced with an identical item."

Stephen Wright's "existentialist" one-liner: "You know that feeling you get when you're leaning back in your chair and you're exactly half way between falling backward and falling frontward? That's how I feel all the time."

This is not really a stand-alone one-liner but the punch line is. Mabel and Walter were in their seventies and Walter was afraid of dying of a heart attack. Before he went in to his doctor for a checkup, Mabel called the doctor aside and said, "Please don't tell Walter if he has a weak heart; it might kill him. Tell me, and I'll break the news to him gently if it's bad news." The doctor agreed, and told Mabel privately after the checkup, "He does have a weak heart, and stress would kill him. So if you want to save his life, you have to obey his every whim, never bitch at him, and agree with everything he says." On the way home, Walter asked Mabel what the doctor said about his diagnosis. Mabel replied, "You're gonna die."

(That punch line has to be given with the voice of Olivia Dukakis in "Moonlighting.")

Anal Jokes

These are "dirty" jokes, but that is quite appropriate because the dirt is only physical, not moral. And it is God's design that every-thing that comes in one end goes out the other. We should certainly not feel guilty about telling such jokes on ourselves. But of course not in polite situations.

A famous Muslim joke is about farts. A proud and successful caliph developed trouble in his digestive tract, and could neither defecate nor even fart. No doctor or laxative could stop the problem, or the pain. The caliph knew this could end only in death. Finally, in desperation, he sent for a Sufi mystic, whom he had always despised but who had the reputation of being very holy and being Allah's instrument for miraculous healings. The caliph offered him half his kingdom if he could heal him. He refused, asking for the whole kingdom instead. The caliph, on the point of death, agreed. The mystic prayed over him and the caliph immediately let out a tremendous fart and knew he was instantly cured. The caliph was about to make good on his promise but the mystic said, "You may keep your kingdom, now that you know its worth." "What do you mean?" asked the caliph. "See for yourself. You sold your whole kingdom for a single fart."

A man complained to his doctor, 'I have an embarrassing problem with farting."

The doctor replied, "That's not a problem. Just buy some Beano and it should stop."

"You don't understand. When I fart, it goes 'Honda!'"

"What do you mean?"

"Listen!" and the man farted and the fart clearly spoke the word "Honda."

The doctor asked: "Are you in the advertising department for an automobile manufacturer, by any chance?"

"No, it just happens to me. What could be causing that?"

The doctor, instead of inspecting the rest of the man's body, looked into his mouth, and said, "Aha. It is as I suspected. You have an abscess in your second molar. Go see your dentist."

"I know I have that dental problem, but what in the world does that have to do with my farting?"

"We don't understand exactly how it works, but I think that if you just see your dentist, that other problem should clear up."

The man left the doctor's office convinced that the doctor was a quack, but saw his dentist anyway. The dentist examined him and said, "You have an abscess in your second molar. Do you have any other problems?"

"Why do you ask? What other problems do you mean?"

"Is there anything strange about your farting?"

"Why, yes, there is. When I fart, it goes 'HONDA!' My doctor said the abscess was the cause, and I thought he was a quack. But you came up with the same diagnosis. That's amazing. How did you know that?"

"It's not amazing at all. Don't you read romantic poetry?"

"This is making less and less sense every minute. What does that have to do with it?"

"I thought everyone knew that. It's a well known cliché that abscess makes the fart go 'HONDA.'"

Many aspiring writers sent their manuscripts to Samuel Johnson, the great curmudgeonly English essayist and literary critic. To one of them, he replied with my favorite negative book review: "Dear Sir: I am sitting in the smallest room in my house, and I have your book in front of me. Soon I shall have it behind me."

If you still think anal jokes are somehow sinful, remember that Saint Paul made a great anal joke in Philippians 3. "If any other man thinks he has reason for confidence in the flesh, I have more: circumcised on the eighth day, of the people of Israel, of the tribe of Benjamin, a Hebrew born of Hebrews, as to the law a Pharisee, as to zeal a persecutor of the Church, as to righteousness under the law blameless. But whatever gain I had, I counted as loss for the sake of Christ…for his sake I have suffered the loss of all things, and count them as refuse." The RSV uses the euphemism "refuse" for the Greek word *skubala,* but the old King James translation is not so delicate and proper. Since *skubala* is the Greek S-word, the KJV uses the word "dung," which of course is the old English s-word.

Here's a silly anal pun that depends on your knowledge of "Star Trek": How is the starship "Enterprise" like toilet paper? It circles Uranus looking for Klingons.

Lawyer Jokes

Law is important. The profession of being a lawyer is an important and honorable one. Why then have there always been so many lawyer jokes, and why are they the most unflattering? Even Shakespeare defined Utopia by "first, we kill all the lawyers." Why?

I honestly don't know. But they are funny, and that's all I have to know to justify them.

A lawyer wakes up from a serious operation to find himself in a hospital room with the blinds totally drawn shut. He asks the nurse why. She says: "Well, there's a big fire across the street just outside your window, and we know you were scared of dying from the operation, so we didn't want you to wake up and think the operation failed and you wound up where you belonged."

A Jew, and Hindu, and a lawyer are walking companions. One night they lose their way in the woods. It's freezing, and they are in trouble. They see a light in the distance. It's the tiny home of a hermit farmer. They knock on the door and wake him up.

"We're freezing to death. Can we sleep in your warm house?"

"Sure. But there are three of you and I only have two beds in the spare room. So one of you will have to sleep in the barn. But it's warm there too."

The Hindu says, "It is my karma. I will do it." So the Jew and the lawyer fall asleep on the two beds. Five minutes later there is an angry knock on the door. It's the Hindu.

"I cannot sleep in that barn. There is a cow in it. Cows are sacred in my religion. If I sleep with a cow that is sacreligious. It makes me unclean."

"Oh, well," says the Jew. "I guess I will have to sleep in the barn." So the Jew goes to sleep in the barn and the Hindu and the lawyer fall asleep on the two beds. Five minutes later there is an angry knock on the door. It's the Jew.

"I can't sleep in that barn. There are pigs in it. Pigs are unclean. I can't sleep with pigs. It's against my religion. It makes me unclean."

"Well, I guess I will have to sleep in the barn," says the lawyer, and he goes to sleep in the barn while the Jew and the Hindu fall asleep on the two beds. Five minutes later there are two angry knocks on the door.

It was the pig and the cow.

What is the difference between God and a lawyer?
God doesn't think he's a lawyer.

What is the difference between a sperm and a lawyer?
One out of every 20 million sperm becomes a human being.

Conversation heard in a bar:
"Lawyers are crooks!"
"You take that insult back! I demand an apology."
"Oh, I'm sorry, sir. Are you a lawyer?"
"No, I'm a crook."

A woman sues a man for defamation of character for calling her a pig. The judge rules in her favor, and the man asks the judge, "Does that mean I can no longer call Mrs. Hogg a pig?" "Yes," replies the judge. "And does that mean I cannot call a pig 'Mrs. Hogg'?" "No, I can't fine you for calling a pig 'Mrs. Hogg.'" So the man turns to Mrs. Hogg and says, "Good afternoon, Mrs. Hogg."

The Devil walks into a lawyer's office.

"What can I do for you, sir?" asks the lawyer politely.

"Oh, no," says the Devil. "It's what I can do for you. I can make you richer than Bill Gates and more famous than Alan Dershowitz. All you have to do it sign this little contract giving me the rights to your eternal soul and the soul of your wife and children and grandchildren and all their descendants for the next thirty generations."

The Devil hands the lawyer the contract. The lawyer narrows his eyes suspiciously, takes the contract, reads every line very carefully, looks up at the Devil, and says,

"What's the catch?"

Question: What's the difference between a lawyer roadkill and a skunk roadkill?

Answer: Skid marks in front of the skunk.

Question: Why do they use lawyers instead of rats for experiments in scientific laboratories?

Answer: Because there are some things rats just will not do.

A lawyer, a priest, and a rabbi are marooned on a raft in the Pacific. They see an island and steer the raft toward it. But a fleet of sharks circles the island, preventing them from landing. The priest says, "They'll eat us if we cross their line. There's only one thing to do. I'll jump in the water on the left side. All the sharks will come to eat me. While they're doing that you two swim ashore on the right side. Better two of us live than none." "No need for that," says the lawyer, and swims right into the middle of the shark line, which parts like the waters of the Red Sea for Moses. "I think we've just seen a miracle," says the priest, as they follow the lawyer ashore. "Nah," says the rabbi; "it's professional courtesy."

A jeweler from New York looking for a bargain is walking through San Francisco's Chinatown. He sees an old, dusty, musty little shop with the old, dusty, musty little shopkeeper sitting on the steps outside the door. The shopkeeper says: "Come in! Come in! You want bargains? Bargains galore here!" The jeweler enters the store and finds it full of gold statues, statues of everything you could imagine: people, animals, buildings. He picks up a gold rat, about a foot long, hefts it in his hand, and says to himself, "This is solid 14 carat gold. It must be worth at least $10,000. I wonder why anyone would put so much gold into a rat." Then he notices the price tag: "Rat, $10; story about rat, $10,000." "What does this mean?" asks the jeweler. "It mean what it say," replies the shopkeeper. "You want rat, you pay me ten dollar. You want story about rat, you pay me ten thousand dollar." "There's a catch, right? You have to take the story to get the rat?" "No, no, but I know you will want to hear story. It is very good story." "Not to me," says the jeweler, plunks down $10, puts the rat under his arm and walks out into the street. "What a bargain!" he thinks. Then he hears the patter of little feet behind him, turns to look, and sees a large rat following him. Then he notices a few more. Then he sees thousands of rats coming out of every sewer, all chasing him. He's terrified. He hates rats. He's desperate. He thinks: "When I was a little kid, my favorite fairy tale was the Pied Piper of Hamelin, where the hero saves the town of Hamelin from the plague of rats by piping them into the sea with the magic golden flute. Maybe there's magic in this gold rat. It's my only chance." He's half a block from San Francisco Bay, so he runs to the water with the rats close behind him and throws the gold rat into the sea. Sure enough, all the rats follow the gold rat and drown themselves. He sits down on the dock, watches the dead rat bodies float past him, tries to figure it all out, struggles with himself for five minutes, finally gives up, goes back to the shop, and finds the shopkeeper on the front steps. "Ah, you come back. I knew you would. You want story about rat, no?" "No," says the jeweler. "Why you come back then?" The jeweler says nothing, enters the shop, and starts looking around everywhere. "What you looking for now?" asks the shopkeeper. The jeweler replies, "I was hoping you had a gold lawyer."

Philosophical Jokes

John was a brilliant boy and got straight A's in every subject, and graduated from Harvard, but he had one serious psychological problem: he thought he was dead. His parents tried one psychiatrist after another, to no avail. Finally, they found one who guaranteed a cure. "But it will cost you a quarter of a million dollars." They were desperate, so they agreed. The psychiatrist took the money, gave it back to the parents, and said, "Enroll him in the best medical school you can find, then come back after four years and I will cure him." So John went to Johns Hopkins for four years and aced every subject. After graduation, John, his parents, and the psychiatrist met in his office for the cure.

"John, what courses did you take in medical school?"

"I took every single one and I got an A in every one."

"So you took a course in anatomy and physiology?"

"Of course."

"So tell me, do dead men bleed?"

"Sometimes, yes, but only shortly after they die."

"What about 25 years after they die?"

"No, that's impossible."

"How old are you, John?"

"I'm 25."

"And how long have you been dead?"

"For 25 years."

"Good. Now tell me, did you take a course in the scientific method as applied to medicine?"

"Yes, I did."

"Tell me how you make a diagnosis."

"Well, the first thing is to look at the data, what presents itself to the senses."

"Good." Now please observe this data very carefully." And the psychiatrist picked up a pin from his desk and stuck it into John's hand. "Tell me what you observe. What data presents itself here?"

"I am bleeding."

"Correct. Now one more question. Did you take a course in logic?"

"I did."

"And did you get a straight A in that course too?"

"Yes, I did."

"All right, now I want you to use your logic to draw the conclusion from these two premises: One, dead men do not bleed. Two, I am bleeding. What conclusion logically follows?"

John stared at his bleeding hand, shocked, and said to the psychiatrist, "Doctor, you are a genius! You have proved me wrong. In fact I have been wrong all my life. Dead men do bleed after all!"

(That's really a logic joke, like the Irish one about the lawnmower. In fact, it's the same fallacy.)

The following joke could be classified as a logic joke because it depends on an ambiguity, but it's really a "let's poke fun at fools" joke.

A 911 dispatcher gets a phone call from a hunter. "We're out in the woods hunting bears, and my friend just collapsed and he's not moving at all. I think he's dead, and I don't know what to do." The dispatcher replies, "We have your location and help is on the way." "But what should I do?" "Well, the first thing to do is put your phone down and make sure he's dead." The dispatcher hears silence, then a shot, then "OK, what next?

This one also could be classified as a logic joke, or as a bar joke, or just as a "clever." A man walks into a bar and says to the bartender, "I'll bet you five hundred dollars I can pee in a shot glass from ten feet away without spilling a drop." "This I gotta see," says the bartender, so both men put five hundred dollars on the bar. The bartender puts down the empty shot glass, the man lowers his pants and pees, and it spills all over the bar. The bartender picks up the money, cleans the bar, and smiles, thinking, "What an idiot." The customer then walks back to a table where a frowning man is sitting, collects something from him, and leaves. The bartender walks over to the table and asks the man, "What did that idiot say to you?" The man replies, "He collected on a bet." "What bet?" "He bet me a thousand dollars he could pee on your bar and you'd just smile and wipe it up."

Another bar joke that could be a logic joke (its point is an equivocation) is perhaps not appropriate for young children because of the slanguage, although when you analyze it there seems to be nothing immoral about it, and it makes everyone smile, especially music lovers. A piano player in a bar is playing all the songs the customers request, and he has a trained monkey who dances on the bar while the pianist plays. The monkey comes to one customer and dips his balls in the martini. The customer, outraged, walks over to the pianist and complains, "Do you know, your monkey dipped his balls in my martini?" The pianist replies, "No, man, but if you hum a few bars I can probably pick it up."

A rabbi, at prayer, received a mystical Enlightenment. Suddenly, all his questions were answered. He ran out into the streets in joy, shouting, "Eureka! I have found it! I have found the light! I have found the answer!" A little boy heard him, and asked, "Rabbi, what was the question?" The rabbi's face fell. "I forgot."

What is the question an aspiring philosopher in college will probably ask more often than any other for the rest of his life? "Do you want fries with that?"

What is the difference between a philosophy teacher and a large pizza? A large pizza can feed a family of four.

A philosopher was out of work and desperate, so he want to the zoo and asked if he could clean the cages. The zookeeper said, "No, but I might have a temporary job for you. Are you a good actor? Can you ham it up?"

"Sure," said the philosopher."

"Well, our gorilla just died and its replacement isn't due for another couple of months. Go rent a good gorilla costume and get in his cage tomorrow and act like a gorilla. If you fool the public you have a job for a few months."

So the philosopher did as he was told, but he fooled nobody and was laughed and hissed at. So the zookeeper said, "You're fired."

"Give me one more chance, please. I have to eat, after all. I'll go ape tomorrow, I promise you."

"OK, one more chance. Tomorrow."

The next day the philosopher really went ape, and everybody was fooled and loved him. But when he climbed a tree the branch broke and he fell into the adjoining cage, which was the lion cage. The lion looked skinny and hungry and began to stalk the philosopher, who huddled in the corner of the cage. He thought:

"I'm a philosopher, so I ought to be able to think logically about this. Let's see: there are only two possibilities. If I don't call out for help I won't lose my job, but I will probably be eaten. And if I do call out for help, I'll certainly lost my job, but I'll probably be rescued and not eaten."

After weighing the consequences and the probabilities, he decided not to risk his life for a job. But it was too late. The lion was right on top of him, and as he opened his mouth to call out for help, the lion put his paw against the philosopher's mouth and whispered in his ear, "Shut up, you fool. You're not the only philosopher out of work."

A logic joke from Lincoln that is relevant to today's transgender controversy: If we call a tail a leg, how many legs does a dog have? Answer: Four. Calling a tail a leg doesn't make it a leg.

St. Peter chains the man and the woman together and says, "That's 100 years for you two."

The man says to the woman, "I wonder what we did to deserve that?"

The woman replies, "I don't know what you did, but all I did was to step on a duck."

Conclusion

G.K. Chesterton is one of the most beloved writers of modern times. Last time I checked, Bartlett's *Familiar English Quotations* listed him more frequently than anyone else except Shakespeare and the Bible. Why are there so many lovers of Chesterton?

The answer is simple: because he makes you happy. He keeps acting even after he's dead, making readers happy.

Why does he make us happy? Because he is funny.

How is he funny? Not by jokes but by turning us upside down, showing us that we were upside down in the first place but thinking we were right side up. That's why all his famous so-called paradoxes are the opposite of what they seem to be. We upside-down people are the real paradoxes. He lets us laugh at ourselves and our popular clichés.

Here is the last and perhaps greatest paragraph from his greatest book, *Orthodoxy*. It is about the funniest and happiest man who ever lived. I cannot possibly do better in ending this poor book than by quoting his great one:

"Joy, which was the small publicity of the pagan, is the gigantic secret of the Christian. And as I close this chaotic volume I open again the strange small book from which all Christianity came; and I am again haunted by a kind of confirmation. The tremendous figure which fills the Gospels towers in this respect, as in every other, above all the thinkers who ever thought themselves tall. His pathos was natural, almost casual. The Stoics, ancient and modern, were proud of concealing their tears. He never concealed His tears;

He showed them plainly on His open face at any daily sight, such as the far sight of His native city. Yet He concealed something. Solemn supermen and imperial diplomatists are proud of restraining their anger. He never restrained His anger. He flung furniture down the front steps of the Temple, and asked men how they expected to escape the damnation of Hell. Yet He restrained something. I say it with reverence: there was something in that shattering personality that must be called shyness. There was something that He hid from all men when He went up a mountain to pray. There was something that He covered constantly by abrupt silence or impetuous isolation. There was some one thing that was too great for God to show us when He walked upon our earth; and I have sometimes fancied that it was His mirth."